W9-BGK-767

GREAT BIBLE
PASSAGES

TREASURES
FROM THE
WORD

DAVID C. COOK PUBLISHING CO.
ELGIN, IL 60120

This Basic Bible Series study was developed through the combined efforts and resources of a number of David C. Cook's dedicated lesson writers. It was compiled and edited by Edward Shewan, designed by Melanie Lawson and Dawn Lauck, with cover art by Richard Sparks.
    —*Gary Wilde, Series Editor*

Great Bible Passages: Treasures from the Word

© 1988 David C. Cook Publishing Co., 850 North Grove Ave., Elgin, IL 60120 Printed in U.S.A.

Scripture quotations, unless otherwise noted, are taken from the Holy Bible: New International Version, © 1973, 1978, 1984 by the International Bible Society, used by permission of Zondervan Bible Publishers.

ISBN: 1-55513-018-6
Library of Congress Catalog Number: 88-70797

Proverbs 8:10

Choose my instruction instead of silver,
knowledge rather than choice gold . . . .

Contents

Words That Stand Out

What makes a Bible passage great? Obviously, every word of the Bible is great—it is the Word of God.

Yet, why is it that some passages, like the loftier peaks of a mountain range, stand out above the rest? Why do our minds turn to Psalm 23 and not Psalm 13? Why, when someone mentions the Book of Genesis, do we almost unconsciously block out the other 49 chapters and think only of chapter 1? Why is Ecclesiastes 3:1-15 our primary link with that book? Why are Romans 8 and I Corinthians 13 loved even by casual Bible readers?

Perhaps part of the answer is that these passages, with exquisite power, bring us face-to-face with what it means to be truly human. They reach a pinnacle of revelation in that they touch us at the deepest parts of our human psyches—our greatest concerns, our most profound joys, our deepest longings. And they show us that God is with us in the midst of each of those poignant human situations, calling us to new levels of spiritual growth.

Doubtless, we need the historical portions of the Bible if we are to learn to live in the future. And we certainly need correct doctrine in order to avoid some fatal mistakes in our thinking about God and His will. But "when life tumbles in" we will no doubt return to our treasure passages for the strength, hope, and comfort we need to meet the challenge with holy confidence.

1
Creating a Good Work

Truth to Apply: Observing God's inventive power unleashed in Creation encourages me to use my own creative potential for His glory.

Key Verse: God saw all that he had made, and it was very good. And there was evening, and there was morning—the sixth day (Gen. 1:31).

"As a younger Christian, I never thought it right to use the word creation for an artist's work. I reserved it for God's initial work alone. But I have come to realize that this was a mistake, because, while there is indeed a difference, there is also a very important parallel. The artist conceives in his thought-world and then brings forth into the external world. This is true of an artist painting a canvas, a musician composing a piece of music, an engineer designing a bridge or a flower arranger making a flower arrangement. First there is the conception in the thought-world and then a bringing forth into the external world. And it is exactly the same with God. God who existed before had a plan, and he created and caused these things to become objective. Furthermore, just as one can know something very real about the artist from looking at his creation, so we can know something about God by looking at his creation. The Scripture insists that even after the fall we still know something about God on this basis" (Francis A. Schaeffer, *Genesis in Space & Time*).

In your opinion, how much can be known of God through nature?

Genesis is the beginning of our physical, as well as our spiritual existence. In this book we encounter the stunning events of the earth's birth as designed by God's creative power and will. Likewise, we see the amazing seed thoughts of our spiritual birth as revealed by God's redemptive power and choice.

God Himself is the subject of Genesis 1, as He is the focus of the chapter. God acted in an orderly manner with specific purposes as He created the earth and its inhabitants. Here God is exalted, not the works of His hand.

Even though Genesis 1 is not a technical scientific treatise, it is an historical document that records the revelation of God. Though some have preferred to view it as more symbolic than chronological in its intent, it is certainly not a mere mythical poem, but rather measured and majestic prose, whose formal style is almost liturgical. God is magnified in this cosmic panorama, that sweeps the visible universe through the eyes of Moses.

Genesis 1 is the foundation of all Scripture and is the historical preparation for human existence. The rest of the book surveys human history from the "birth" of Adam until the death of Joseph. The first half of the book (1:1—11:26) is the "primeval history," which is divided into five sections introduced by the phrase "This is the account of . . ." (2:4; 5:1; 6:9; 10:1; and 11:10). The second half of the book (11:7—50:26) is the "Patriarchal history," which is likewise divided into five sections (11:27; 25:12; 25:19; 36:1, 9; and 37:2).

The Creation narrative of 1:1—2:3 forms the introduction to the primeval history as well as to the whole Book of Genesis. God performed His work in six days. The first three days were for giving form to the formless, and the next three days were for creating things to fill the emptiness. With each day, God, in His infinite wisdom, made known more of His divine order of things, fulfilled His plan, and finally evaluated His work. "God saw all that he had made, and it was very good." On the seventh day, our Creator rested from all His labor.

Light on the Text

The Conception of His Work (1:1-3)

The first verse in the Bible states in concise, majestic words the story of Creation. God is the Creator who spoke the universe into existence. The Gospel of John starts with the same words: "In the beginning," stressing the activity of Jesus Christ in Creation. Not only is Jesus our Redeemer, He is also our Creator. In fact, all three persons of the Trinity were active in Creation from the beginning (Gen. 1:1, 2; Jn. 1:3, 10).

"Create" is a special verb in the Bible, which always has God as its subject and never human beings. But we as His creatures are able to use our minds to make or form or fashion from the substance of the earth. However, God has created *ex nihilo* ("out of nothing"), as confirmed in Heb. 11:3: "By faith we understand that the universe was formed at God's command, so that what is seen was not made out of what was visible." The material universe was made solely by the creative Word of God. Therefore, the major premise of the Bible is "In the beginning God created the heavens and the earth." We must begin our study by believing this truth, then—on this foundation—we can ruminate on all the rest of Scripture.

Verse 2 describes the world in its elementary form. If God had not spoken, the earth would still be formless, empty, and dark. The phrase "formless and empty" is a rhythmic, catchy phrase in Hebrew (*tohu wa-bohu*) which opens up the structure of the rest of this first chapter: in days 1—3 God separates and gathers, giving form to the earth; in days 4—6 He fills the emptiness with various good things. The Spirit of God is depicted as hovering over this chaotic situation, perhaps contemplating what He is going to do next. In the same way, the Holy Spirit comes upon us and sees the darkness and chaos in our own hearts. Accordingly, we might ponder the question, "What kind of good work does He want to create in me?" (see Ps. 51:10).

The Commencement of His Work (1:4-25)

The first day of Creation (vs. 3) begins with a pure

symbol of God Himself: light. God said: "Let there be light." He simply has to speak and light appears. God's words are so powerful that His thoughts are remarkably transformed into reality. From a human point of view, light seems appropriate to create first. Since no one can work in the dark, I must first turn on the light so I can begin my undertaking.

Likewise, my spiritual life begins with "the light of men" (Jn. 1:4). Jesus is the light that shines into the darkness of my soul, convicting me of my sin and rebellion against God. He wants to make me a "new creation" (II Cor. 5:17). Therefore, I must cry out like the Psalmist of old: "cleanse me from my sin . . . create in me a pure heart, O God" (Ps. 51:2, 10).

Moses wrote the Creation story in chapter 1 from the point of view of God's glory. The word "God" is repeated *over* 30 times in this chapter. He is always the subject of the sentence. God is the central figure of creation. He is Creator, the Author of Life, and Ruler of Creation. God is the subject and mankind is the object. God is the Sovereign Lord and man is the object of His glory. Practically speaking, this means God is the Lord of my life, the Lord of my family and the Lord of my nation. God has given me this most precious gift of life, to be lived out during this appointed time.

In the second day of Creation (v. 6), God separated the waters by the expanse of the atmosphere. The waters above the expanse relate to the source of precipitation and clouds. The waters below would become the seas, oceans and rivers on the third day, as the waters were gathered and dry ground appeared.

Our Creator established signs in the sky to mark off periods of time on the fourth day (vss. 14, 15). These heavenly bodies that illuminate the earth have several purposes: (1) to govern the day and the night, restraining the "darkness [that] was over the surface of the deep" (vs. 2); (2) to determine the "seasons" of the year, thus regulating human, animal, and plant life on the earth; (3) to calculate the "days" and "years," making human history possible; (4) to shed light upon the earth for its substance. Our knowledge today of the sun as a source of energy helps us appreciate the present effect of God's magnificent creative activity on the fourth day.

Fish and birds were the main events of the fifth day of Creation (vs. 20). God created a great abundance of aquatic life. Not only were the seas "teeming with creatures beyond number" (Ps. 104:25), but they were also filled with a variety of species. "The great creatures of sea" no doubt includes the "leviathans" of Old Testament poetry, as described in Job and Psalms (Job 7:12; Ps. 104:26; 148:7). Perhaps insects could also be included with "every winged bird" in verse 21 (cf. Deut. 14:19, 20). God graciously cares for the animals by blessing them and making it possible for them to "be fruitful and increase in number" (vs. 22).

The Climax of His Work (1:26, 27)

We now reach the pinnacle of God's creative activity. On the sixth day, God created animals and humans. We were formed in the "image" of God. How are we like God? Certainly not in a physical way, since God is spirit. The "likeness" is essentially in spiritual terms. Our spiritual personality includes many characteristics that distinguish us from the natural world in which we live. Like God, people are created with moral and intellectual capabilities. They are able to reflect on themselves and their circumstances. They can choose a source of action because they each have a will. People can express love and communicate with others, and they can be creative, like their Creator, bringing form and design with purpose to the world around them.

The Completion of His Work (1:31; 2:1-3)

Having created the universe and an earth in which human beings might happily live, God looked at what He had accomplished. Each day of Creation had already ended with the satisfaction of a job well done; now God reflects on all He has created and declares it "very good." This good implies the total absence of evil—no flaws, errors, or weaknesses. All things in their proper place, they are able to fulfill their God-given role.

On the seventh day, God rests from all His labor, taking pleasure in all He has done. This rest is not like our physical repose, which is needed to regain stamina and strength. Rather, it is a self-satisfaction in what He

13

had done, appreciating the beauty and wholeness of the world He had created. God's rest is an active, rational exercise of contemplation and meditation.

In this act of resting, God established a precedent for everyone who engages in creative work. He extends His own pleasure to Creation itself, blessing it and making it holy, so that the whole earth might know the peace of God. This day of rest, instituted as a constant reminder on the Sabbath, points ultimately to the final rest when all God's people will be present, joyfully worshiping Him in the new heavens and earth (Rev. 21).

For Discussion

1. How does God's creative power, which was unleashed at Creation, effect your life today?

2. In light of Phil. 1:6, what "good work" do you visualize God creating in you?

3. What can we learn from God's example for our own creative pursuits?

4. List some practical ways you or your group might begin to creatively glorify God.

Window on the Word

A Christian, above all people, should live artistically, aesthetically, and creatively. We are supposed to be representing the Creator who is there, and whom we acknowledge to be there. It is true that all men are created in the image of God, but Christians are supposed to be conscious of that fact, and being conscious of it should recognize the importance of living artistically, aesthetically, and creatively, as creative creatures of the Creator. If we have been created in the image of an Artist, then we should look for expressions of artistry, and be sensitive to beauty, responsive to what has been created for our appreciation.

(Edith Schaeffer, *Hidden Art*)

2
Who Cares?

Truth to Apply: As I learn to depend on my Shepherd-God, I am free to graciously meet the needs of another.

Key Verse: The Lord is my shepherd, I shall not be in want (Ps. 23:1).

A poor child who lived in the slums of London many years ago is said to have wandered far from home one day. Her mother was sick and the little girl was distraught over her mother's condition. In her bewilderment she lost her way and wandered into a part of London where she obviously had never been before. She came to a great fenced-in area more like a garden than a yard. A beautiful young lady was walking inside. However, what most captivated the poor child was the unbelievable variety of colored flowers. The idea struck her that perhaps she could trade something for a flower to cheer up her sick mother. "Please, Miss," she said. "I wonder if you would trade for a flower." She held out her small token of exchange. Without a word the young woman inside began to pull up flower after flower. The child's eyes widened as she saw the ever-increasing bouquet. "You don't mean you're going to sell me all those flowers for this one thing," she stammered.

"Don't be silly," the young woman replied. "My father doesn't sell flowers. My father is the King of England. He loves to give them away."

Our Heavenly Father provides profusely, so the believer may echo "my cup runneth over." Share a time when you received one of God's gracious gifts.

F. B. Meyer calls Psalm 23 "an oasis in the desert . . . a grotto in a scorching noon . . . a sequestered arbour for calm and heavenly meditation." Even though it contains just over a hundred words, Psalm 23 is in effect the holy of holies among the Psalms. Henry Ward Beecher proclaimed, "The Twenty-third Psalm is the nightingale among the Psalms. It is small, of a homely feather, singing shyly out of obscurity: but it has filled the air of the whole world with melodious joy. . . . Blessed be the day on which that Psalm was born! (Quoted by James Stalker, *The Psalm of Psalms*.)

A number of Bible commentators believe that the (vignette) picture in Psalm 23 shifts at verse 5 from that of Shepherd with sheep to one of host with guest. In this regard Stalker points out that in his adolescence David was a shepherd in the pastures near Bethlehem (I Sam. 16:11; 17:20), while in his adulthood David was a sovereign in the palace at Jerusalem. As a King, David would frequently have entertained guests at his table (II Sam. 9:5-7, 10-13). Just as David provided for his dependents, so the Lord cares for the needs of His sheep. This is the heart of Psalm 23.

Light on the Text

Provision (23:1-3)

In Genesis 48:15, Jacob, who was near to death, spoke of "the God who has been my shepherd all my life to this day." Both Jacob and David use the same metaphor or picture of God as one who herds sheep. Jesus Himself claimed, "I am the good shepherd. The good shepherd lays down his life for the sheep" (Jn. 10:11). Matthew 9:36 says, "When he saw the crowds, he had compassion on them, because they were harassed and helpless, like sheep without a shepherd." He is the One who cares for the people: calling, leading, nourishing, and protecting, even if it costs Him His life. Jesus calls us by name, and we recognized His voice; He knows us and we know Him

(Jn. 10:3, 14). God desires to have this same intimate relationship as a shepherd has with his sheep.

Verse 2 amplifies why sheep "shall not be in want." There is ample food and water for the flock. A Scottish shepherd once quizzed Donald G. Barnhouse concerning the behavior of sheep. Barnhouse recalls, "He asked me if I had ever seen a sheep eat while lying down. If a sheep is lying down . . . even though there is a lovely tuft of grass within an inch of her nose, she will not eat it" (*God's Heirs*). Hence a sheep that will "lie down" is fully fed. The shepherd leads the sheep "beside quiet waters." F. H. Wight cites that "sheep are apt to be afraid of drinking water that moves quickly, or that is agitated" (*Manners and Customs of Bible Lands*).

In verse 3 it becomes more apparent that the metaphorical sheep involved is a person. Human sheep need "soul" restoration and direction in "the paths of righteousness." Correction ("restores") and direction ("guides") are two major needs of God's sheep. The psalmist conveys similar thoughts in Psalm 119:

(1) A deterrent if one sins: "How can a young man keep his way pure? By living according to your word" (Ps. 119:9).

(2) A deterrent from sinning: "I have hidden your word in my heart that I might not sin against you" (Ps. 119:11).

These are main requests in the Lord's Prayer, though in reverse order: "And lead us not into temptation, but deliver us from the evil one" (Mt. 6:13). Therefore, if you need to have your soul restored to, or routed along the right paths, the Good Shepherd gladly complies.

Protection (23:4, 5)

Although this is a pastoral vignette, all is not pleasant in this chapter. God's sheep have enemies, in this present life (vs. 5) as well as the last enemy: death (I Cor. 15:26). "The valley of the shadow of death" (vs. 4) seems less vicious than it might be because the sheep do not travel alone. Comfort comes not only from the shepherd's personal presence but also from his accompanying equipment. The shepherd carries a rod and a staff.

"Rod" most probably refers to a stout, stocky club

around three feet long, that may have "had a knobbed end which was studded with nails or flint" (Stigers, *Wycliffe Bible Encyclopedia, II*). The Hebrew word for "rod" is used not only of an instrument for beating (Ex. 21:20), but also for counting sheep, for example, "Every tenth animal that passes under the shepherd's rod" (Lev. 27:32).

The second Hebrew word, translated "staff" in Psalm 23:4, refers to a walking cane (Ex. 21:19; Ezek. 29:6; Zech. 8:4). The shepherd's staff has many possible uses as cited by Mackie: "It is help in clambering over rocks, in striking off leaves and small branches, in chastising loitering sheep and fighting goats, and on it the shepherd leans as he stands" *(Bible Manners and Customs)*. In addition, a shepherd's staff does not necessarily contain a crook at the top of the cane, as frequently portrayed.

The stage seems to shift from a shepherding scene, (vss. 1-4), to that of a host and guest. The question that arises is: Can a person enjoy a banquet surrounded by enemies? In the ancient Middle East, if a fugitive was on the run and managed to get to a friendly sheikh's tent, his pursuers could not harm him. Though he might be within death range of their knives, as far as the unwritten rules went, he was safe. David had been involved on more than one occasion in such a chase, fleeing like an outlaw, yet God protected and provided for him (cf. II Sam. 17:1, 27-29).

The anointing of a guest's head with oil was a common Eastern courtesy, as witnessed in Mary's anointing Jesus' head in Mark 14:3. Likewise, the shepherd lovingly applied soothing olive oil to the sores and scratches on his sheep. Most certainly, God showed his favor by symbolically anointing David with oil. God's blessing was also depicted by David's overflowing cup.

Prospect (23:6)

Perhaps the psalmist is writing from the vantage point of his seasoned years of later life, for he speaks in verse 6 of being followed "all the days of my life." As he assesses his past as one being in the care of his Shepherd-God, he stands assured that "goodness and love" will accompany him the rest of his days. "Goodness and love" are like twin companions who are welcome pursuants compared to his enemies in verse 5. "Goodness" refers to something that is pleasant, moral, beneficial and generous, all attributes of God from which the word "good" has its origin. "Love," on the other hand, refers to a "covenant love" that reflects the kind of binding loyalty existing between two parties who have some form of agreement. Thus, the psalmist knows that God has obligated Himself in loyalty to the child of His covenant.

In the last phrase in verse 6, David yearns for the day when he will "dwell in the house of the Lord forever." Though he lived prior to the building of the Temple, David visualized, planned, and prepared for that glorious day. And yet in his heart was a longing for "the greater and more perfect tabernacle that is not man-made" (Heb. 9:11, 24); to be in the presence of his Shepherd-God forever.

For Discussion

1. For David, God demonstrated His love and goodness in a tangible way. How has God provided for and protected you in the past?

2. The imagery of the Shepherd restoring a lost sheep to the fold, or guiding the flock along a mountain path portrays the way Christ Jesus influences us in our personal lives. Has the Lord been convicting you of something in your life that does not please Him? How has God directed you lately in a business decision, family matter, or personal goal?

3. There are times in our lives when death casts a shadow over our path. How does God help us overcome fear and anger and loss when a loved one passes away? What is your experience with grief?

4. Fear is a powerful emotion that grips our hearts, especially in the presence of our enemies. Do you experience God's comfort, protection, and acceptance even when your "foes" are threatening your well-being (I Jn. 4:18)?

Window on the Word

On Sunday, a certain pastor declared the glory of Heaven in his sermon. One of his wealthy members was moved by what he said, but was curious about the exact location of Heaven. So, the next morning the parishioner met his minister and remarked:

"Pastor, you preached a good sermon about Heaven. You told me all about Heaven, but you did not tell me where Heaven is."

"Ah," said the pastor. "I'm glad for the opportunity this morning. I have just come from the hill yonder. In that cottage there is a member of our church who is extremely poor; she is sick and in bed with a fever. Go and take her a good supply of provisions and say, 'My sister, I have brought these provisions in the name of our Lord and Savior.' Then ask for a Bible and read Psalm 23, and after that get down on your knees and pray. If you don't see Heaven before you get through, I'll pay the bill."

The following morning our opulent friend returned to his pastor and reported, "Pastor, I saw Heaven, and I spent fifteen minutes there on my knees. Believe me it is true, as certainly as I am standing before you."

Jesus Christ is our Shepherd-Pastor who prepares a place for us in eternity. But He also wants us to taste a bit of Heaven in our present lives. He has richly blessed us in every way, and desires that we in turn go and become a blessing to someone in need today.

3

Time Management

Truth Apply: In reflecting on how I use my God-given resource of time, I am compelled to constantly reevaluate my priorities.

Key Verse: He has made everything beautiful in its time (Eccl. 3:11).

"Next to grace time is the most precious gift of God. Yet how much of both we waste. We say that time does many things. It teaches us many lessons, weans us from many follies, strengthens us in good resolves, and heals many wounds. And yet it does none of these things. Time does nothing. But time is the condition of all these things which God does in time. Time is full of eternity. As we use it so shall we be. Everyday has its opportunities, every hour its offer of grace" (Henry E. Manning, *The New Book of Christian Quotations*).

What is typically the biggest "time waster" in your daily routine? How do you deal with the problem?

The theme of Ecclesiastes is the haunting refrain: "Utterly meaningless, Everything is meaningless. What does man gain from all his labor at which he toils under the sun?" (1:2, 3). The "Teacher" searches for meaning in life, but he finds it as illusive as "chasing after the wind" (1:14). He seems torn over the shallow strivings of humanity in light of God's matchless Sovereignty.

The structure of this Book is a series of quests on the part of the authors, exploring various avenues of life for meaning. The "Teacher" studied wisdom, pleasures, toil, oppression, advancement, riches, and civic obedience. In each case, he could find nothing of permanent value. Though he begins his exploration from a secular point of view, he concludes that fearing God and keeping His commandments is the only way to find meaning in all our toil under the sun.

According to Derek Kidner, "The function of Ecclesiastes is to bring us to the point where we begin to fear that such a comment (1:2) is the only honest one. So it is, if everything is dying. We face the appalling inference that nothing has meaning, nothing matters under the sun. It is then that we can hear, as the good news which it is, that everything matters—'for God will bring every deed into judgment, including every hidden thing, whether it is good or evil.'

"That is how the book will end. On this rock we can be destroyed: but it is a rock, not quicksand. There is a chance to build" (*A Time to Mourn, and a Time to Dance*, InterVarsity Press).

Light on the Text

Times and Seasons (3:1-8)

From birth to death, through the natural seasons, in and out of the various human emotions, and through the highest and lowest of mortal activities, "there is a time for everything." By means of fourteen anonymous couplets, the "Teacher" describes the endless ebb and flow of our moods and actions as dictated by the tyranny of time.

"A time to be born and time to die" depicts the entirety of one's earthly existence, the beginning and end of which we have no control. Within this limited framework, all the activities of planting and harvesting crops, of butchering and healing livestock, of destroying and building structures, fill our every waking moment to meet our basic needs for food and shelter.

Verse 4 expresses the contrasting sentiments of human emotion. There is a time for weeping and mourning at the loss of a loved one, the ruin of rejection, the despair of deception. Ralph Waldo Emerson observed that "sorrow makes us all children again, destroys all differences of intellect. The wisest knows nothing" *(The New Book of Christian Quotations,* compiled by Tony Castle). Likewise, there is a time for laughing and dancing, when our hearts are overflowing with the joy of a new-born baby, the sunshine of a child's smile, the hilarity of a humorous tale, the gaiety of a wedding feast.

"A time to scatter stones" refers to the custom in the days of Israel for an invading army to gather stones on their march and throw them into the enemy's field, making it impossible to plow or cultivate. On the other hand, the people would gather the stones out of the field to make it usable, as well as to build walls and other structures.

"Embracing" is a sign of love, respect, or comfort and support. But there are times we have to refrain from embracing, exerting the discipline to withdraw from the pleasurable in order to meet a higher priority—a duty, for example, that calls us away from our loved ones.

"A time to search" or pursue implies active, voluntary obtaining, usually in business with respect to property or merchandise. In contrast, there is a time to relinquish those possessions or commodities. As one commentator states, "the collector disperses his hoard." There is a time for maintaining and caring for what is already in one's possessions, while there is another time for voluntarily throwing off one's belonging. We are reminded of Jesus' words "Whoever loses his life for me will find it" (Mt. 16:25).

"A time to tear" probably refers to the Jewish custom

of tearing garments during the time of mourning, and then, after the ritual period was over, sewing up the tear so that the garment was once again whole. Some scholars see in this verse a reference to discord and unity in a community or nation as well.

Knowing when to speak and when to be silent is an art, that is sought after by the prudent. For example, Job's friends came and sat with him in silence for seven days, sharing his grief without trying to talk him out of it (Job 2:13). Jesus, on the other hand, told Paul, "Do not be afraid; keep on speaking, do not be silent" (Acts 18:9). Solomon wisely summarized this couplet in the following adage: "The lips of the righteous know what is fitting, but the mouth of the wicked only what is perverse" (Prov. 10:32).

Finally, in verse 8 we return to the most general categories of human emotion and activity. On the individual level, there is "a time to love and a time to hate." However, when these affections are transposed to the social level, there comes "a time for war and a time for peace."

What can we learn from this list of times and seasons? First, that time is not in our hands, because God has set an unchangeable divine order. We can do nothing to change what He has established. Our task is to recognize these appointed times and seasons in a spirit of cooperation with the Master's design.

Secondly, we recognize that the way of the world is not left up to fate or chance. There is a divine order at the heart of the universe, not chaos. God set the heavenly bodies in space to govern the day and night, the times and seasons, for all humanity. These times will reach "their fulfillment," when all things will be put into submission to Christ (Eph. 1:10).

The Meaning of It All (3:9-13)

The "Teacher" begins this lesson by asking what the worker can expect to gain from all his hard work. His answer initially is described as a "burden" that is God-given, which becomes "beautiful" at God's appointed time. Furthermore, God has put eternity in our hearts, which creates within us a longing to see the whole context of life—not just the fleeting moments. "We are like the desperately nearsighted, inching their way along some great tapestry or fresco in the attempt to take it in. We see enough to recognize something of its quality, but the grand design escapes us, for we can never stand back far enough to view it as its creator does, whole and entire, 'from beginning to end' " (Kidner).

God has given each of us work to do, work that is demanding yet rewarding. Perhaps we need to recall that God gave Adam work prior to the Fall. Far from being a punishment, work was a vital ingredient in a fulfilling happy life. Therefore, our happiness depends upon us yielding to God's sovereign will for our role in life, as well as releasing our tight grip on worldly priorities and status symbols, because eternity has been placed in our hearts.

As we recognize that God's will is partly hidden from us, we can exercise the trust in His character and timing that will bring us into closer harmony with Him.

Verse 13 is not to be taken to mean that we should seek pleasure at cost to our neighbor, nor is it an Epicurean "eat, drink, and be merry, for tomorrow we die" kind of fatalism. Rather we are to appreciate the beauty of all things God has created, take advantage of the pleasures God offers us through our work and relationships, and peacefully live in harmony with the order God has ordained.

When the product of our work glorifies God and pleases us, we can surely say we enjoy life.

God's Sovereignty (3:14, 15)

We know that God controls the past, the present, and the future. He is above time, not bound by it as we are. We cannot add to, or subtract from God's plans. They have been from the beginning, and His time is moving towards a grand fulfillment.

Our response to this knowledge of God should be a holy fear, a reverential awe that recognizes supernatural power and might. Think of it—He who governs our lives also has complete control over all aspects of the universe, from the complex system of galaxies to the structure of atoms visible only under a microscope. We fear, yes; but we can also trust and rest confidently in such a God. His righteousness is unchangeable; He is a holy God who personally cares about us as we move along in the stream of life He has created.

Finally, because of His holiness and righteousness "God will call the past to account" (3:15). There is also an appointed time for judgment, where every thought, word, and deed will be examined. Even the secret things will not be overlooked by the piercing eye of God. Therefore, in the final analysis, life is not utterly meaningless, a chasing after the wind; rather, it is utterly meaningful because "God will bring every deed into judgment, including every hidden thing, whether it is good or evil" (12:14).

For Discussion

1. Since there is "a time" for everything under the sun, list specific ways from your everyday life that you are controlled by time.

2. Our life's work seems to be a burden at times, and yet it has its rewards—even for the most mundane tasks. How do you visualize God making your work ultimately beautiful? satisfying?

3. Though we cannot fully fathom God's design, He has placed a sense of eternity in our hearts. How does this hope encourage you in your active schedule?

Window on the Word

The Clock of Life

The clock of life is wound but once,
    And no man has the power
To say just when the hands will stop;
    At late, or early hour.

Now is the only time we own
    To do His precious will,
Do not wait until tomorrow;
    For the clock may then be still.

4

We Shall Overcome!

Truth to Apply: When I grow weak to the point of despair, I can rely on my incomparable Creator to renew my strength.

Key Verse: Those who hope in the Lord will renew their strength. They will soar on wings like eagles; they will run and not grow weary, they will walk and not be faint. (Isa. 40:31).

Ben Johnson of Canada ran the 100 meter race in a record breaking 9.83 seconds, beating the world record of 9.93 set by Calvin Smith in 1983. Johnson boasted "This record might last for 50 years. . . . If anybody's going to break it, they're going to have to beat me, and my first 50 meters are awesome." Charlie Frances, Johnson's coach, believes the Jamaican-born sprinter can even break the 9.8-second barrier, once thought to be physically impossible.

Yet the Scriptures say: "Even youths grow tired and weary, and young men stumble and fall" (40:30). Although we can attain great feats of human strength, we must humbly acknowledge our own limitations. At times we feel broken and useless, in desperate need of even one drop of God's strength. As Moody used to say, "the only way to keep a broken vessel full is to keep it always under the tap."

In what ways has God been able to use you even at your weakest, most vulnerable times?

The great prophet Isaiah lived through a pivotal period of Judah's history. The Northern Kingdom of Israel fell in 722 B.C., and the ten tribes of the north were captured. King Uzziah's rule of Judah came to an end, as well as a 50-year peace from foreign aggression. The rest of the century was dominated by Assyrians ambitious for empire exploits. Isaiah's ministry continued approximately from 740 B.C. to 680 B.C., about sixty years—the longest of any of the prophets.

The book written by Isaiah is "recognized as the literary masterpiece of all Hebrew writing" (J. W. Watts, *Old Testament Teaching*). This "prince of prophets" is quoted more by New Testament writers than any other Old Testament book: 590 references from 63 chapters are found in 23 New Testament books. Irving Jensen has said that, like the whole Bible with its 66 books, Isaiah has 66 chapters. These are divided into two basic sections, like the Old and New Testament divisions. Isaiah 1—39 emphasizes divine condemnation, whereas chapter 40—66 stress divine consolation, a pattern that reminds us of the wrath of God and grace of God in Scripture (*Survey of the Old Testament*).

Chapter 40 emerges from the far different world of Hezekiah's in chapter 39, into the waning days of Babylonian captivity a century and half later. The next eight chapters reflect an air of liberation from human bondage by Cyrus the Great of Persia, and from spiritual bondage through the promised Servant, the Light to Gentiles. Judah was on the eve of destruction and deportation, and would suffer seventy years of exile. Therefore, Isaiah delivers prophetic words of comfort and hope. If God's people were to trust Him unreservedly for help in times of distress, they would have to learn to depend on His powerful attributes.

Light on the Text

The Matchless Supremacy of God (40:18-24)

The second half of chapter 40 is a lesson made up of

questions; the main one is "To whom will you compare God? To an image? Who is His equal?" (see 40:18, 25). This is followed by the chiding interrogative: "Do you not know? Have you not heard?" (40:21, 28). Then the chapter closes with an answer to the implied questions: "Does God truly care about me? Can I trust Him?"

To start with, the people needed to remember the utter futility of trusting in the gods of Babylon. Many Mesopotamian deities were represented by idols made of gold, silver, and wood. Pagan practices had gained quite a foothold among God's people. Consequently, Isaiah poured out biting sarcasm upon the idol worshipers (40:18-20), then countered with four rhetorical questions (vs. 21) to emphasize that Yahweh is Sovereign over all things.

Verses 22 and 24 answer the questions. In picturesque language, they call our attention to the unmatched image of God. As a king sits upon his throne, so God dwells in the highest part of the earth to watch over all that goes on there. In contrast, the earth's inhabitants are compared to "grasshoppers," which are numerous and powerless like the fragile human race. We did not create the world, nor can we hold it on its course. As E. J. Young comments, "And if grasshoppers cannot do it, how much less anything that is made by grasshoppers?" Furthermore, are not the princes and rulers part of this same humanity? They, too, are no greater than a seed that is planted, takes roots and is blown away by the whirlwind. The Lord God Almighty is Sovereign over all He has made.

The Mighty Strength of God (40:25-28)

Verse 25 echoes the language of verse 18, except that the prophet was the speaker in the earlier passage. Here the speaker is God Himself, who virtually declares, "there is nothing in the universe equal to me."

According to verse 26, the God who created the heavens is also the Shepherd of the stars. The true lesson from the majestic procession of the stars is that God is in precise control of the entire universe. The Hebrew phrase "to bring them out" carries the idea of counting them one by one. Young notes that this term is used elsewhere of military matters (cf. II Sam. 5:2; Isa. 43:17).

Young states that "God has assigned to each member of His army its particular nature, characteristics, and function." Because of divine power, not one star is missing. The thought seems to be that God has more than enough power to keep each star on its appointed course. He calls forth the heavenly bodies and keeps them in their appointed places.

The people of God were complaining (vs. 27) that God had forgotten about them. The verb used here implies a constant complaining. We are reminded that sometimes we display a similar attitude in times of adversity. We are the ones who have forgotten about God. He is our all-powerful Creator, who shepherds not only the universe, but our personal lives, as well.

"Do you not know? Have you not heard?" (vs. 28). The prophet inquires, "Have you not learned that God is Creator from the foundations of the earth?" The apostle Paul echoes the same thought in Romans: "For since the creation of the world God's invisible qualities—his eternal power and divine nature—have been clearly seen, being understood from what has been made, so that men are without excuse" (1:20).

Even though the people of Judah would be held in captivity in the near future, it was God who was in control, not only of the universe, but also nations and rulers. Human authorities are subject to God, and He can remove them from positions of power at will. God never grows weary. No one can fathom God's purposes; even much searching cannot bring total understanding of the infinite God.

The Meek Sufficiency of God (40:29-31)

In the preceding verses God seems somewhat aloof, but Isaiah makes it clear that God is indeed concerned for our frailties in these closing verses. God promises to bestow power on His children when they are about to falter. He is there to help us meet the strenuous demands of life.

We who know Christ realize that supernatural strength comes through the Holy Spirit, the "Helper" who comes alongside us to help us. The phrase "increases power" does not mean to simply add strength, but to multiply or to give power in abundance. In contrast, the most outstanding athletes reach the end of their endurance, and stumble and fall. Therefore, the Spirit of God who never grows weary promises to renew our strength.

"Renew their strength" implies an exchange or substitute for something better. Our life is like a single thread or wire, which in and of itself is fragile. But when many threads or wires are twisted together they become a strong cable. So, the moment we exchange our threadbare strength for God's power, and twist our lives around our mighty Creator, we will become energized once again. We will sprout wings like eagles, defying gravity, and begin to fly. Before we were too weak to take one more step, but now the incomparable strength of God empowers us to run and not become exhausted, to walk and not languish.

For Discussion

1. We do not worship idols made of wood and precious metals in the twentieth century. However, what "idols" have crept into your life lately, that have robbed God of His rightful place in your heart? How do they compare to God Himself?

2. How does the knowledge of God's eternal attributes— transcendence, sovereignty, omnipotence and omniscience—encourage you when you are feeling down?

3. There is absolutely no one equal to our eternal Creator. When was the last time you looked into the heavens at night and stared at "the starry host"? Our God is truly powerful, placing each heavenly body in space, and holding the universe together. Discover one new aspect of God's creation today. How are God's eternal power and divine nature clearly seen in that aspect?

4. At times we feel our lives are so insignificant compared to God Almighty, that perhaps God has

forgotten about us. How does Isaiah help you overcome this faulty notion? What weakness are you willing to exchange for the mighty strength of the Lord?

Window on the Word

Why Not Trust God?

A motorist speeding down a highway sees another car approaching on a road that will intersect the highway at a right angle; but seeing a red stop sign for the driver of the other car, the motorist continues his speed, confident that he is safe. He thereby exercises complete faith in an unknown person not only to see the stop sign but also to heed its warning. . . .

There are countless acts in our daily lives that are based on a blind and unquestioning faith. This faith is placed in the integrity and honesty of our fellowman.

(From "What's Happened to Our Faith?" by Elizabeth F. Koop, *Eternity*, March, 1972)

5
Satisfaction Guaranteed

Truth to Apply: God is calling me to leave my spiritual poverty and to seek His abundant mercy and pardon. All I have to do is say, "Yes!"

Key Verse: Seek the Lord while he may be found; call on him while he is near (Isa. 55:6).

"A great monarch was accustomed on certain set occasions to entertain all the beggars of the city. Around him were placed his courtiers, all clothed in rich apparel; the beggars sat at the same table in their rags of poverty. Now it came to pass that on a certain day one of the courtiers had spoiled his silken apparel so that he dared not put it on, and he felt 'I cannot go to the King's feast today for my robe is foul.' He sat weeping till the thought struck him, 'tomorrow when the king holds his feast, some will come as courtiers happily decked in their beautiful array, but others will come who will be dressed in rags, and be made quite as welcome.' 'Well, well,' said he, 'so long as I may see the king's face and sit at the royal table. I will enter among the beggars.' So without mourning because he had not his silken habit, he put on the rags of a beggar and he saw the king's face as well as if he had worn scarlet and fine linen.

"My soul has done this full many a time when her evidences of salvation have been dim and I bid you do the same when you are in like case: if you cannot come to Jesus as a saint, come as a sinner; only do come with simple faith to Him and you shall receive joy and peace."
(From *The Best of C. H. Spurgeon*, Baker)

Background/Overview: *Isaiah 55:1-9*

The Book of Isaiah is a powerful book, which uses rich metaphors and imaginative language. Isaiah's writing possesses a lyricism that is unmatched, that scales lofty heights (chs. 40, 53, 55). J. Sidlow Baxter rightly declares, "what Beethoven is in the realm of music, what Shakespeare is in the realm of literature, what Spurgeon was among Victorian preachers, that is Isaiah among the prophets."

As a prophet, Isaiah seems to have enjoyed high social status. He was well-known in the courts of Kings Ahaz and Hezekiah. He wrote accounts of the reigns of Uzziah and Hezekiah. His writings bear the stamp of a well-educated man. Isaiah was married and had two sons, Shear-jashub ("a remnant will return") and Maher-Shalal-Hash-baz ("quick to plunder, swift to the spoil").

The kings that ruled during Isaiah's ministry were Jotham, Ahaz, and Hezekiah. Jotham followed in the godly footsteps of his father Uzziah. However, Ahaz was a wicked king who encouraged Baal worship and infant sacrifice. He also pursued a pro-Assyrian policy, which proved a desperate move and showed lack of faith. When King Hezekiah came to the throne, Assyria was on the doorstep to the north and Judah was ripe for revival. He was a God-pleasing king who opened the doors of the Temple once again, cleansing all signs of Baal worship. Though he honored the Lord, the people committed all kinds of gross sins of idolatry and injustice. Against these sins, Isaiah raised his voice as God's spokesman.

Light on the Text

A Free Offer (55:1-3a)

In perspective, chapter 40 reveals God's offer of salvation, through the imagery of warfare ended and the coming Shepherd Lord. Chapter 53 tells of the "Suffering Servant," by whose death salvation would be appropriated. Chapter 54 recounts the blessing that the suffering Savior would obtain for His people. And Chapter 55 is a call addressed primarily to Israel, but applied more broadly to people everywhere.

Verse 1 is rich in Middle-Eastern imagery and spiritual significance. The hunger and thirst plaguing the people suggest a felt need among the people—a craving for God. Where water is a precious and scarce commodity, it is sold in some countries by a vendor who guards his wares. In Isaiah's mind, water, milk, and wine represent spiritual nourishment and refreshment of the Lord. J. P. Lange observes that the wine and milk were a costlier and nobler means of nourishment than water. "Milk is the wine of infancy, wine the milk of maturity" (*Commentary on the Holy Scriptures: Isaiah*).

"And you who have no money, come, buy and eat! Come, buy wine and milk without money and without cost" (vs. 1). A free offer! All I have to do is reach out and take freely from God's gracious hand. In these words of Isaiah the New Testament concept of God's grace was foreshadowed. As Paul put in his letter to the Ephesians, "For it is by grace you have been saved, through faith—and this not from yourselves, it is a gift of God" (Eph. 2:8). Verse 1 simply states, "all things are ready; the guests are invited; and nothing is required of them except to come" (Keil and Delitzch).

We find a pattern here in verse 2 that runs through much of the writings of the prophets; namely, a conversation between the Lord and His people. In Isaiah 1:18, God sits down together with His people and urges "come now, let us reason together." The people are directed in Isaiah 55:2 to weigh their priorities and values. They had spent hard-earned money for bread that did not satisfy. So, God offered them a choice: to continue in their ways of malnutrition, or listen to Him and indulge in gourmet delights. The choice seems ludicrous, and yet we, too, find it difficult to accept God's incredible offer of grace.

"Give ear" (vs. 3) means to listen by shutting out competing noises and focusing on a specific sound or voice. Step two is "come to me"—"Come near to God and he will come near to you" (Jas. 4:8). If we "hear" what God is trying to tell us then we will receive the promise that our souls will live. Rozell observes, " 'Your soul' refers to the totality of one's being, the entire self, not simply to that part of the individual which continues after death."

The Agreement (55:3b-5)

The covenant idea is very prominent in the Old Testament. Israel was God's covenant people; therefore, when the concept of covenant was mentioned, it had special meaning which was understood.

Isaiah's emphasis was that the free offer in the preceding verses were as sure as the Covenant made to David. In other words, behind the invitation to the thirsty was the assurance already made with David that God would fulfill His Word. To the people of Isaiah's time this would have helped to prove that God had not forsaken them.

David was an inspiration—the least son of Jesse who became a great warrior King. Psalm 89:3, 4 asserts, "I have made a covenant with my chosen one, I have sworn to David my servant, I will establish your line forever and make your throne firm through all generations." A kingdom had been promised for David, a realm that would last forever. Isaiah said that this solemn promise would be fulfilled as proof of God's "faithful love" to Israel.

Verse 4 has a dual meaning in that it looks back toward King David, and forward to David's greater Son, the promised Messiah. There are numerous Old Testament statements containing allusions to the Messiah in David's name (cf. Ezek. 34:23; 24:37; Jer. 30:9; Hos. 3:5).

Verse 5 has a missionary tone. The Messiah, the seed of David, would not only redeem His people Israel; He would also call nations who do not know Him. The verb "hasten" indicates the effectiveness of the call; when the Gospel is proclaimed, these nations will come running to the Messiah. This verse looks forward ultimately to a time when God will be known throughout many nations.

The Terms of the Agreement (55:6, 7)

One of the greatest invitations to trust and obey God in the Bible is found in verse 6. The essence of His appeal is that of a father who longs for the return of his way-ward children. "God is reaching out His hand; that must be grasped. God is seeking man; man must seek the Lord" (Leupold). God waits patiently, "not wanting anyone to perish" (II Pet. 3:9). But God may not always be available. "How unspeakably important then it is to seek for mercy at once," pleads Barnes ". . . lest we be removed to a world where mercy is unknown!" The apostle Paul echoes the same plea to the Corinthians: ". . . now is the time of God's favor, now is the day of salvation" (II Cor. 6:2). "How shall we escape if we ignore such a great salvation?" (Heb. 2:3).

We find here clear evidence that God is a God of forgiveness and compassion, ready to give His wayward children yet another chance. These are very generous words, for they speak about God's loving-kindness toward undeserving "wicked" and "evil" ones, even ourselves. Isaiah knew how rebellious his country had become. Do we recognize how evil our own country has become? Even the waywardness of our own souls?

Verse 7 is "the Gospel in miniature," for it contains the elements of God's plan of salvation. First God calls us to repentance ("Let the wicked forsake his way and the evil man his thoughts"). We must turn away from our rebellion against God; then turn to God in faith ("let him turn to the Lord . . . and to our God"). At that time God promises forgiveness of sins ("and he will have mercy on him . . . he will freely pardon"). Repentance, faith and forgiveness are essential terms of this eternal Agreement God has made with those who are spiritually thirsty and receive His free offer of grace.

The Guarantor (55:8, 9)

God's way of dealing with the human race defies understanding. Why should a holy God invite sinful people to seek fellowship with Him? His ways and thoughts are put in opposition to the ways of the wicked and the thoughts of the evil ones (vs. 7). Therefore, as Edward Young observes, "The sinner must forsake his own ways, because his ways are not those of God." Barnes believes that verses 8 and 9 are connected to the preceding verses by the subject of pardon. Human beings find it difficult to pardon; they may harbor malice and seek revenge. But God is not reluctant to forgive. The mercy and compassion of our Heavenly Father are supernatural. He is the almighty Guarantor to this amazing Agreement which is beyond our humble imagination: Satisfaction is guaranteed!

For Discussion

1. Have you ever been so thirsty or hungry you thought you would faint? In what ways do you "hunger and thirst" for righteousness (Mt. 5:6)?

2. What have you been spending your money on lately that does not quench your inner thirst? How might you redirect your energy to satisfy your inner hunger?

3. The Lord made a covenant with David, an everlasting agreement, which is open to all people. How can you "summon the nations" to follow God in your own community? Choose one person to tell about God's "free bread offer."

Window on the Word

God Is Near

A secular philosopher once asked a Christian, "Where is God?" The Christian answered, "Let me first ask you, Where is He not?"

God is near. Call on Him!

6
The New Covenant

Truth to Apply: I am called to move into an intimate, inward relationship with God.

Key Verse: I will put my law in their minds and write it on their hearts. I will be their God, and they will be my people (Jer. 31:33).

The Thirty Years War had brought a flood of refugees into the besieged city of Eilenberg, Saxony. Widespread fever broke out, taking more than 8,000 lives.

With the sick and dying all about him, Martin Rinkert, the only clergyman in Eilenberg, labored until he was ready to drop from exhaustion. But when the sickness finally abated, a widespread feeling of thanksgiving rose in many hearts. Thus, Rinkert was moved to write a hymn to mark Eilenberg's deliverance:

Now thank we all our God
    With heart and hands and voices,
Who wondrous things has done,
    In whom His world rejoices;
Who, from our mothers' arms,
    Hath blessed us on our way
With countless gifts of love,
    And still is ours today.

Rinkert, like Jeremiah, had broken through the dark night of sorrow with a message of hope and joy. Have you ever experienced such a "break through"?

Background/Overview: *Jeremiah 31:27-34*

R. K. Harrison (in *Jeremiah and Lamentations*) sets the stage for the woebegone scene in which Jeremiah lived and wrote:

"It has been correctly observed that, at times of great moment in the history of His people, God has called men of outstanding spiritual stature to guide the nation according to the divine will and to foster a vision of its destiny as the Chosen People. Jeremiah was one of those summoned to discharge this important task, made all the more difficult by the continued state of political and religious crisis in the Southern Kingdom (Judah) during his ministry. The prophet spoke at a time when the ancient Near East was in an almost unparalleled state of ferment. Within his lifetime he witnessed the collapse of the mighty Assyrian empire and the rise of a virile Babylonian regime that swept across the Near East and battled the powerful Egyptian armies to a standstill. In his own country he experienced a succession of political crises, interspersed with only the briefest periods of hope for national stability. As the moribund Assyrian empire relinquished its grasp upon former spheres of political influence, the Southern Kingdom enjoyed a welcome period of independence and freedom from external control. This respite, however, ended all too quickly when Egypt endeavored to assert its former power in Palestine and Syria. As though subjugation of this kind was not enough, Judah was compelled to exchange a bad master for an even worse one when the Babylonian and Chaldean armies brought an end to the existence of the Southern Kingdom by a relentless depopulation of the land. The various agonizing crises through which the nation passed are clearly evident in the utterances of one of Judah's most loyal sons (Jeremiah). . . ."

Amid the bleakness of this period in Hebrew history, Jeremiah issued a most welcome bit of news—that God would someday supplant the Sinai Covenant with an inner covenant of the heart.

Light on the Text

A New Anticipation (31:27, 28)

What better news could come to a broken and divided
people than Jeremiah's announcement in these verses?
The Lord was promising to reverse His actions toward
His wayward people. Not just toward the Northern
Kingdom (Israel) or the Southern (Judah), but toward
His people as a whole. God declared that "the days are
coming" when He would repopulate this beloved, yet
devastated, land with livestock and people. This is a very
"earthy" passage. The language here suggests that God
would cultivate His people as a farmer tills his soil:
plant, uproot tear down, build. R. K. Harrison observes:
"Once the lessons of apostasy have been learned, the
heavenly Sower will increase the productivity of the
people and their flocks in a bustling, thriving land."

   Jeremiah has revealed the sovereignty of the Creator
and Destroyer of all things according to His will.
Through his foreshadowing of things to come, Jeremiah
reminded the people of God's unlimited power both to
bless and to curse, as He chooses. Though God had
obviously dealt firmly with His people, yet He is willing
to renew a right relationship with them. We see in these
verses the forgiveness of God, the power of God, the
determination of God. He was not happy to let Israel
die. He would not destroy them forever.

A New Accountability (31:29, 30)

The saying mentioned here shows that the Jews in exile
had done a very understandable, human thing: blamed
their parents ("The fathers have eaten sour grapes") for
the problems they were facing ("and the children's teeth
are set on edge"). Dr. Harrison observes that this
"reflected the skepticism of the exiles (Lam. 5:7; Ezek.
18:1), who felt that God was judging them unjustly for
circumstances which were no fault of theirs. Jeremiah
repudiates this idea, showing that in the future, people
will be punished for their own sins. Ezekiel 18:3, 4
amplifies this same theme of individual moral
responsibility."

People were saying that their country had been laid waste, their family and relatives killed or broken up, and they were exiles in a distant heathen land because in their generation God had chosen to punish the nation for many generations of evildoing—of neglecting God and disobeying His will. They felt bitter because they were "taking the rap," so to speak, for what their ancestors had done.

How like today! We often hear people blaming their parents—or other circumstances over which they have minimal control. The problem is that each generation invariable repeats the sins of the previous generation, perhaps with ingenious variations. There is indeed conditioning toward sin by both heredity and environment. But the guilt is properly placed by God with the individual sinner, who must bear direct personal responsibility for all he or she has done (or not done) to displease God, break His holy Law, and violate His marvelous grace.

A New Agreement (31:31-34)

The Old Covenant, which stood behind Jeremiah's promise of a New Covenant, came about through God's giving of the Law to Moses (Ex. 19, 20). From that time until the days of Jeremiah, God alone had kept the Covenant faithfully—His chosen people had broken it again and again. In brief moments of remorse and repentance, they had returned to it. But soon they would break faith again. Indeed, this is a substantial part of Old Testament history.

The time of reckoning came in Jeremiah's day. Having used less radical means of jarring His people out of their sinfulness, God finally allowed heathen armies to destroy the city of Jerusalem and kill or bring many Jews into bitter captivity far from Jerusalem (see Ps. 137).

Yet this great national disaster was not the end for God's chosen people; it was simply a bitter interlude on the long, torturous pathway leading from the Old Covenant, to the New.

The reference to God as "husband" (vs. 32) suggests that the relationship between God and His people paralleled a marriage. The entire Book of Hosea draws upon this analogy. God is represented by the long-suffering husband, Hosea, whose wife, Gomer, symbolic of the chosen people, is unfaithful. This is further developed in the New Testament by the apostle Paul in Romans 7:1-6 and Ephesians 5:23-32.

The New Covenant, Jeremiah declared in verse 33, would not be a matter of rules, nor outward signs. Instead, God, through the New Covenant, would make His precepts known to each believer. Instead of stone tablets, God would inscribe His Law upon the inner person. Human will, mind, emotions, and intentions would be yielded to God. The New Covenant of internal change would replace the Old Covenant of outward signs and rules. It would no longer be necessary constantly to teach people to know God. For this would be second nature, like breathing and sleeping. And all who knew God in this intimate way would have their sins forgiven.

Although Jeremiah did not spell out all the details of timing for the New Covenant, other portions of Scripture make it clear that the Covenant was fulfilled in Jesus Christ. He alone puts people into a new and right relationship with God. He alone is the means of the New Covenant—a fact we celebrate in the Lord's Supper: "Then he took the cup, gave thanks and offered it to them, saying 'Drink from it, all of you. This is my blood of the covenant, which is poured out for many for the forgiveness of sins" (Mt. 26:27, 28).

THE OLD AND NEW COVENANTS COMPARED

The Old	The New
given through Moses	came through Christ
written on stone tablets	written on their hearts
a list of rules (Law)	a living relationship (Grace)
sin recognized	sin removed
bears fruit for death	bears fruit to God
symbolized by circumcision	represented by the Spirit and water
preparatory	complete
no power to save	"the power of God for the salvation of everyone who believes" (Rom. 1:16)

43

For Discussion

1. Are you willing to acknowledge Jesus as Lord in your life? If He truly is in control of your existence, in what ways has He been "uprooting" you because of your rebellious attitudes and actions? How is He "replanting" you in the soil of hope?

2. At times we all have accused our parents of eating "sour grapes" and feel we are unjustily suffering for what they did or did not do. Have you been harboring any angry thoughts toward your mother or father? What could you do to begin a process of reconciliation? (See Mal. 4:5, 6 and Lk. 1:17.)

3. Most Christians sincerely desire to know God intimately. Yet at times we become uncomfortable when Jesus "comes near." We want to run away like Jonah, or give up like Elijah, or ask our older brother to help us like Moses. In what ways has the presence of God made you feel uncomfortable lately? What might you do to regain intimacy with the Lord Jesus?

Window on the Word

Internal Life

Dr. Walter Wilson was visiting in a home, where each of the members of the family were asked to quote a Bible verse. One little girl quoted John 3:16 as follows: "For God so loved the world, that He gave His one and only Son, that whoever believes in Him, shall not perish but have INTERNAL LIFE."

Needless to say, Dr. Wilson did not correct her because God's love for us is not only for eternity, but He also desires the intimacy of "internal life" now. Jesus told His disciples, "If anyone loves me, he will obey my teaching. My Father will love him, and we will come to him and make our home with him" (Jn. 14:23).

7

Lawsuit: God vs. Israel

Truth to Apply: Heeding God's outrage against the unethical practices of His people, I am compelled to reevaluate my attitudes and actions toward others.

Key Verse: What does the Lord require of you? To act justly and to love mercy and to walk humbly with your God (Mic. 6:8).

In _Les Miserables_ Victor Hugo tells of a bishop who was assigned to a 60-room mansion. Across the street from the bishop's mansion was a six-room hospital. One day the bishop crossed the street and asked, "How many patients have you here?" He was told 26 patients. "In six rooms?" the Bishop asked. "Yes," they said. "We are very crowded."

"Obviously there has been some mistake," said the bishop. "You shall have my house, and I will take yours. Move your patients."

So the sick people were moved into the 60-room mansion, and the bishop moved into the little one-story hospital. However, the people in the town were amazed and disturbed. "He doesn't act like a bishop," they gossiped.

But, as the Reformer Ulrich Zwingli said: "A Christian's task is not to talk grandly of doctrine, but always to be doing hard and great things with God."

What "hard and great thing" have you seen God accomplish through you or someone you know?

Micah prophesied at a time (735 to 700 B.C.) of general prosperity in Judah. The leadership of King Uzziah had brought the nation to an economic plateau that had not been enjoyed since the time of Solomon. This prosperity, however, was not without problems. The political scene was threatening. The leading nation of that time, Assyria, invaded Israel during Micah's lifetime. The northern Kingdom fell to the Assyrians during this period.

The social conditions described by Micah were deplorable. The poor and widows were oppressed (2:1, 2, 8, 9). There were false prophets who controlled the people and who prophesied for money (2:11; 3:6, 11). The judges took bribes (7:3).

The religious activity of the people was formal, but not personal. Hezekiah initiated reforms that led to the restoration of the feasts and sacrifices. Idols and heathen altars were destroyed (II Chr. 29—31 describes this period). These reforms did not seem to impress Micah. He viewed them as "window dressing" that did not reflect changed hearts. This condition is addressed in the passage studied now.

Light on the Text

The Case *(6:1, 2)*

The opening of this chapter indicates that God had a charge to make against Israel, a charge based on the people's rebellion against Him in turning to other gods and in their failure to live up to the standards God required. The setting is much like a law court with a dialogue between God and the nation.

The Charge *(6:3-5)*

In verse 3 God asks two questions. The first—"What have I done to you?"—established God as the offended party in these proceedings. He was in the right and could inquire without fearing that any true answer could stand against Him. God had been fair, just, and merciful in His past dealings with the nation, and any true answer to this question would underscore His goodness.

The second question is very disturbing—"How have I burdened you?" The verb "to burden" has the idea of exhausting someone's patience. This could be by failing to keep promises or making too heavy demands. God could not be accused of either. His faithfulness is certain, and His requirements are not burdensome.

God went on to invite the people to bring their charges, as He said "Answer me." He was willing to hear what the people wished to say. Clearly He could not be accused legitimately. He had not forgotten His people nor His promises to them. The evidence was all on God's side, and He began to present it, beginning with the Exodus.

The first words of verse 4, "I brought you up," are a play on words. The Hebrew for "I brought you up" and "I burdened you" is very similar in sound, and there is implicit in this phrase the idea that not only had God not burdened His people—He had in fact delivered them. The deliverance from Egypt was so signifcant in the nation's history that it is almost always referred to in any description of Israel's past. This event is always described as an evidence of God's love and concern for His people (see Isa. 63:11-13).

God not only brought the people up from Egypt, He also redeemed them from their place as bond servants. They were bound to the Egyptians, and God paid a price for their deliverance.

By God's grace, provision was made for leadership of the nation: Moses, through whom was given the Law; Aaron, the first of the priestly line; and Miriam, a prophetess—all examples of the kind of persons who were going to lead the nation.

Likewise, protection was made for their journey from Shittim to Gilgal: God confounded Balak King of Moab by using Balaam, whom the king hired to curse Israel, to bless them and to declare triumph over their foes.

The Rebuttal (6:6, 7)

This section opens with the way the prophet attempted,

on behalf of the people, to answer the Lord's indictment. The answer begins in verse 6, where the quality of offerings is emphasized. In verse 7 both quantity and quality are in focus. In both cases the people completely misunderstood the requirements of God on their lives.

Verse 7 begins with a question, "Will the Lord be pleased with thousands of rams?"—perhaps a reference to the mammoth offerings presented by Solomon (see I Ki. 3:4; 8:63). These were not personal offerings but were state occasions, and doubtless given at public expense.

The prophet then suggested, with a touch of sarcasm, that the people might offer "rivers of oil." Oil was a part of every offering and the addition of oil raised the value of the offering in the eyes of the giver. But rivers of oil?

Then the value of the offering was raised to the ultimate as the prophet—in great exasperation—asks, "shall I offer my firstborn for my transgression?" In some of the nations around Israel, sacrifice of children was a part of pagan worship. (See Lev. 18:21.) This was a practice for which the Canaanites were condemned before the Israelites invaded the land. Two of Judah's wicked kings—Ahaz and Manasseh—sacrificed their children (II Ki. 16:3; 21:6). The two words translated "transgression" and "sin" make it plain that there was real guilt before God.

Micah's biting words show that he was fully aware of the spiritual bankruptcy of the nation. The people would be willing to bargain with God as if He were some earthly judge who could be bribed. If one thing would not satisfy Him, then perhaps another would.

The Response (6:8)

The people had failed to live up to God's requirements—not because they were ignorant of His standards, but because they chose to ignore them. The people had plainly been told what was required—"He has showed you, O man" (vs. 8). The contrast is striking. In the preceding verses we see that the people tried to build a case by pleading ignorance. But then God told them that they knew what was required of them.

God will not allow us to substitute the offering of

"rivers of oil" or "thousand of rams" for the offering of ourselves. God wants His people to lead lives worthy of fellowship with Him. One who has this relationship must live it out in everyday situations. Three specific areas are mentioned:

"To act justly." Followers of God are part of a community of believers. God calls everyone in that company to practice justice in their relationships. Acting justly involves the negative: a prohibition of bribery, oppression, false witness, and a host of other acts that should not be part of the behavior of God's followers. Acting justly also has its positive side: responsibility towards persons in need, upholding the rights of others, and involvement in actions for the community good.

The second requirement is "to love mercy." Mercy is withholding rightly deserved punishment. God's provision of salvation is an act of mercy. People, in their dealings with others, should reflect the mercy they have been shown.

The third requirement is to walk humbly with God. A life of fellowship with God is to be sought rather than a life of selfishness and self-direction. The proper attitude toward God and His direction brings a daily life in submission to the leadership of God.

Walking humbly does not mean a life of self-abasement. It means a life that is concerned so much with God that self is not selfishly indulged. It is that type of walk that Paul urges in Ephesians 5:15-17.

Note that verse 5 does not teach that a person is made right before God by fulfilling the three requirements of verse 8. Micah was addressing those who already had a relationship with God. He said, "Walk humbly with *your* God." This verse does not outline the way *to* God, but the way in which one who has already found God should live.

The Violations (6:9-12)

In these verses, God has outlined some of the sins of the people. The voice of the Lord heard in the city would bring fear to the wise man, since the Lord expressed disapproval of the actions of the people. The word "rod" usually is synonymous with judgment that has been

49

appointed by the God of Israel.

God's cry against the people is the subject of verses 10-12. According to verse 10 the condemnation came because of two related offenses. The first was that the people had apparently prospered because of their wickedness. But the treasures of wickedness would bring judgment upon those who had accumulated them.

The second phrase of verse 10 is a condemnation of corruption in business. Merchants were accused of using a scant measure to cheat the unwary and to oppress the poor. The words "short ephah" refer to a measure that was scantier than it should have been. The ephah was a dry measure, somewhat smaller than a bushel. Cheating of this kind is an abomination in God's eyes. Amos wrote against the same practice in his prophecy: "Hear this, you who trample the needy . . . skimping the measure" (Amos 8:4, 5).

Businessmen in Micah's day felt that they could divide their lives into two mutually exclusive compartments—the secular and the religious, with one not necessarily connected with the other. God pointed out that they were mistaken. The question "Shall I acquit a man?" (vs. 11) is rhetorical. The answer is obvious. Such people were not honest. God would not let them cheat without punishment.

The Verdict (6:13-16)

Because Micah's people had abandoned the Biblical standards of morality and had given themselves over to dishonesty and deceit, God had brought destruction and ruin upon them in order to bring them to repentance. God was not passive in the face of such practices. His judgment was sure. The people of the nation of Israel had sinned, and God would act. Their material success would be terminated as they were carried away into captivity—the result of God's judgment.

The Lord promises depression to their agricultural economy, and consequent shortages and famine. Later, the nation would be subject to invasion and slaughter at the hands of the enemy. Plenty and possessions will turn into poverty and plunder.

For Discussion

How would you rate yourself/church (from 1 to 10) on this "ethical audit"? Discuss.

____ pilfering items from work
____ fudging on income taxes
____ standing up for the rights of another
____ proper treatment of employees
____ buying stocks in controversial companies
____ caring for the widows
____ finding jobs for the unemployed
____ meeting the needs of the elderly
____ food pantry/clothes supply for the poor
____ taking a stand on social issues like abortion

Window on the Word

A Christlike Conscience

When persecution and evil began to spread through Germany, I looked first to the universities, the great free centers of learning, for opposition. They were soon wiped out. Then I looked to the press, the newspapers and magazines of wide circulation and great power. They were soon suppressed. It was only in the Christian Churches and Christian pulpits that men dared to stand up for the right and truth and freedom.
  (Albert Einstein)

8

What Kind of Person Are You?

Truth to Apply: A new spiritual birth comes through faith in God's Son, who was sent for my salvation.

Key Verse: For God so loved the world that he gave his one and only Son, that whoever believes in him shall not perish but have eternal life (Jn. 3:16).

Dr. C. Everett Koop, the U.S. Surgeon General, thought he was a Christian because he had grown up in a Christian home. Then one morning he wandered into the balcony of Philadelphia's Tenth Presbyterian Church and heard Donald Grey Barnhouse give his usual little explanatory talk before he read the Scriptures. Koop recalls:

"He was about to read the tenth chapter of Hebrews, and he was explaining the fact that Jesus Christ was a priest after the order of Melchizedec. That annoyed me for two reasons. One, I had read the New Testament through and couldn't remember even reading Melchizedec's name. Secondly, I had enough reverence for Jesus Christ so that it bothered me to hear Him called a priest because I knew one priest whose life didn't strike me as being like Christ. . . .

"My wife was pregnant with our third child and not able to attend the services. I went home and told her everything I learned each week. Sometime during the next six months, we accepted the fact that we were sinners, that we were totally lost, and that salvation was by grace alone" (From *Moody Monthly*; May, 1980).

Share your own conversion experience. How did you come to accept Christ as Savior?

Background/Overview: *John 3:1-21*

John pursues his aim of showing that Jesus is "the Christ, the Son of God" (20:31) mainly by seven "signs" and seven "discourses" prior to the Last Supper. The first sign was turning water into wine, and here we have the first discourse concerning the new birth. This was a private talk to a single listener, Nicodemus, a member of the ruling class.

Leon Morris comments: ". . . Nicodemus would have stressed the careful observance of the Law and the traditions of the elders. For the loyal Phrarisee this was the way of salvation. John uses this conversation to show that all such views are wide of the mark. Not a devout regard for the Law, not even a revised presentation of Judaism is required, but a radical rebirth" (*The Gospel According to John*, Eerdmans).

Light on the Text

An Honorable Person Visits Jesus (3:1, 2)

Nicodemus was a spiritual and political leader among his people. As a Pharisee he went through rigorous training, memorizing some of the Pentateuch and studying (what would later be codified as) the Mishnah and Talmud. Through vigorous discipline he had climbed to this respected position of a Pharisee. Likewise, Nicodemus was a member of the Jewish ruling council called the Sanhedrin. The two main requirements to be one of these 70 elite members was education and wealth. Nicodemus had made it to the top. He was now a man of standing, both in religion and politics, a highly honored man in his own country.

Why did such a successful man come to visit Jesus? He seemed to have everything a man could desire: position, power, and possessions. Verse 2 tells us that he addressed Jesus saying, "Rabbi, we know you are a teacher who has come from God. For no one could perform the miraculous signs you are doing if God were not with him." He came to Jesus because of the miraculous signs. He desired this same kind of power in his own life to fill the emptiness that success and wealth could not satisfy.

A Clever Person Questions Jesus (3:3-8)

Long ago the Lord counseled Samuel: "The Lord does not look at the things man looks at. Man looks at the outward appearance, but the Lord looks at the heart" (I Sam. 16:7). Jesus saw the deep need in the heart of Nicodemus: the need for the Kingdom of God. He had all the things that this world could offer, and yet his spirit was filled with anxiety and despair. Nicodemus needed to see the Kingdom of God, and receive eternal life. But the condition was that he had to be born again.

"Born again" is a popular phrase used by many people who say many things about its meaning. The apostle Paul described it as dying and rising to new life with Christ (see Col. 2:20; 3:1). Likewise, the apostle Peter declares, Jesus "has given us new birth into a living hope through the resurrection of Jesus Christ from the dead" (I Pet. 1:3). Therefore, Jesus is offering Nicodemus eternal hope, in contrast to his temporal hope in things of this world.

Nicodemus was a clever man, and immediately realized that Jesus must mean something else other than physical birth. It is ridiculous even to imagine entering a second time into your mother's womb to be born! Jesus explains: "No one can enter the kingdom of God unless he is born of water and the Spirit" (3:5).

Water is spoken of prominently in Scripture. It was used in Old Testament times in ceremonial washings, and in the New Testament Jesus washes the disciples' feet (Jn. 13). The Jews practiced ceremonial washing before meals. And, of course, water became an important Christian symbol after the ministry of John the Baptist. Obviously, water has a cleansing quality that the apostle Paul attributes to the Word of God: "Christ loved the church and gave himself up for her to make her holy, cleansing her by the washing through the word" (Eph. 5:25, 26).

In Hebrew, as in Greek, one word can be variously translated as wind, breath, or spirit. So it is that the word "wind" in verse 8 can be translated "Spirit." What a powerful metaphor! Notice the word "breathed" in Genesis 2:7—"the Lord God formed the man from the dust of the ground and breathed into his nostrils the breath of life, and the man became a living being." The Spirit breathed life into us when we were formed. According to John 3, the Spirit brings us new life so that we might be transformed.

In verse 7 Jesus said, "You should not be surprised at my saying, 'You must be born again.'" Apparently the look on Nicodemus's face was one of incredulity!

Just as the wind blows in a mysterious pattern, the Spirit moves, unseen, among people. We see the evidence. But as the wind is illusive, so, too, the Spirit defies the analysis of natural human understanding (vs. 8). Only as we are reborn in Christ do we begin to perceive with spiritual understanding.

A Proud Person Doubts Jesus (3:9-15)

Nicodemus came seeking answers. Although lacking in understanding and somewhat hesitant, he dared to come to Jesus. (As a member of the Sanhedrin, where Jesus was not popular, he no doubt had some qualms about having anything to do with Jesus.)

In verse 9 Nicodemus pursued his questioning of Jesus about the New Birth, and Jesus chided him for not understanding so basic a doctrine. Yet He left no doubt as to the *necessity* of the New Birth.

Jesus spoke with authority and candidness. "We" in verse 11 may refer either to the Godhead, but more likely refers to the family of true believers, which contrasts with "you"—those who are spiritually callous.

Verse 13 testifies that only the Son, who came from the "Father's side" (Jn. 1:18), has the true picture of God and the true understanding of God's plan for the ages.

Verse 14 compares Christ to the brass serpent with healing powers in the story in Numbers 21:6-9. The serpent was (originally) no idol; it was a symbol graphically presenting God's plan to save obedient people. So, too, the Son, when lifted up on Calvary's cross, would save many. The brass serpent represented the death sting of the fiery serpents. Christ on the cross represented the sting of death for sin. The Son of Man would bear our sins so all who come to Him in faith might receive everlasting life.

A Wise Person Will Believe Jesus (3:16-21)

What can one say about John 3:16 except, in wonder and in awe, praise God for the countless numbers who have received its message of love? It is almost certainly the most familiar and widely memorized verse of the Bible. No child is in Sunday School very long before learning this great verse. The complete message, at once simple and profound, is direct from the heart of God. His purpose is clear; He intends to save His lost and disobedient creatures. Here, in a single sentence, His plan is revealed.

Notice the key words in verse 16: "God," "Son," "gave," "life." They say it all!

Although Christ is the "righteous Judge" (II Tim. 4:8), He did not come in judgment. He came to rescue. God's purpose is not to condemn, but to redeem. To believe or not believe God's Good News is the ultimate question; there is no neutral ground. To be neutral is to fall on the side of unbelief.

God opened the door of faith. All who enter pass "from death to life" (Jn. 5:24). In other words, the transfer of God's unconditional forgiveness to us takes effect the moment we come to Christ. Apart from Him, we have no hope of escaping the awful penalty.

Ever notice how light reveals all? The pure white light of Christ reveals the evil in the world. Who can stand in that pure and perfect light? Nicodemus's real problem was his sin problem. He loved the world so much that he would do anything to get the things of this world.

The point is, all of us shun the light of a righteous Christ. Even as Christ is the light, Satan is the prince of darkness. Satan distorts truth and deceives his followers but he cannot compete with the power of the pure light of the Savior.

Verse 21 stresses the importance of living by the truth. Doing is as important as knowing. James said, "Do not merely listen to the word, and so deceive yourselves. Do what it says" (Jas. 1:22).

One distinct difference between Christianity and other religions is that Christ was not a man who merely claimed He had the truth. He came not to teach us *about* truth, nor to point us *toward* the truth. He said, "I am . . . truth" (Jn. 14:6). Accordingly, one who does the truth is one who belongs to Christ and lives in Him.

For Discussion

1. After looking at the accomplishments of Nicodemus you may have been reminded of your own. How have you become successful in the eyes of your family and friends?

2. Jesus looked right past Nicodemus's outward appearance, into his heart. What would Jesus see if He looked into your innermost being?

3. In verse 19 Jesus said the verdict is that people loved darkness instead of light. But if you live by the truth, what kinds of daily "deeds" would reflect the "Light" that is in you? (Be very practical as you answer.)

Window on the Word

For God So Loved Comrade Captain

Richard Wurmbrand relates a story that illustrates the power of Christian love:

"With about thirty other Christians I remember being in a prison cell in Rumania. One day the door was opened and a new prisoner was pushed in. It took us a little time to recognize him in the half-darkness of the cell. When we did recognize him we were amazed to see not a fellow Christian but a well-known Captain of the Secret Police who had arrested and tortured many of us. We asked him how he had come to be a fellow prisoner.

"He told us that one day a soldier on duty had reported that a twelve-year-old boy, carrying a pot of flowers, was asking to see him. The Captain was curious and allowed the boy to enter. When the boy entered he was very shy. 'Comrade Captain,' he said, 'you are the one who arrested my father and mother, and today is my mother's birthday. It has always been my habit to buy her a pot of flowers on her birthday—but now, because of you, I have no mother to make happy.'

" 'My mother is a Christian and she taught me that we must love our enemies and reward evil with good. As I no longer have a mother, I thought these flowers might make the mother of your children happy. Could you please give them to your wife?' . . . .

"The Captain took the boy's flowers and embraced him with tears in his eyes. A process of remorse and conversion began. In his heart he could no longer bear to arrest innocent men. He could no longer inflict torture. In the end he had arrived with us in prison because he had become a defender of Christians . . . ."

(Richard Wurmbrand, *Underground Saints*)

9

God's Glory Generates Unity

Truth to Apply: Only as the glorious truth about God is made known to me by Jesus will the love of Christ be evident in my oneness with other believers.

Key Verse: I have made you known to them, and will continue to make you known in order that the love you have for me may be in them and that I myself may be in them (Jn. 17:26).

On March 23, 1743, when Handel's *Messiah* was first performed in London, the king was present in the great audience. It is reported that all were so deeply moved by the "Hallelujah Chorus" that the whole audience, including the king, rose to its feet, and remained standing through the entire chorus. From that time on it has always been the custom to stand during the chorus whenever it is performed. With spontaneous joy the souls of all believers stand in solidarity to salute Him who "comes in the name of the Lord." He is the "King of Kings, and Lord of Lords" and with one voice we glorify His Name!

   Can you remember a time in your life when you felt compelled to offer spontaneous praise to God?

Background/Overview: *John 17:1-26*

Within the Gospel of John there is a sizable section, John 13—17, that may seem like a long parenthesis. Earlier chapters offer a narrative that builds with dramatic interest as it recounts the events that lead to Jesus' arrest and trial. At this point the Gospel writer slows the narrative to deal in some detail with incidents and conversations that took place in the Upper Room.

It was here that Jesus washed His disciples' feet (13:1-20), predicted His betrayal by Judas (13:21-30), and foretold Peter's denial (13:36-38). It was here that Jesus gave His disciples a new commandment (13:31-35) and comforted them with assurances that He was the way, the truth, and the life (14:1-14). He promised them the presence of the Holy Spirit (14:15-17, 25, 26; 15:26, 27; 16:5-15), assured them of His closeness to them, as a vine to its branches (15:1-11), and told them that even though they would experience persecution (15:18-25) and grief at His departure (16:19-24), they should take heart because He had overcome the world (16:29-33).

The words of Jesus in this section are often referred to as His "farewell discourses." They were directed to His friends in the intimate atmosphere of the Upper Room. They were intended not only to answer specific questions but also to prepare the disciples for the time of testing soon to come. As John tells the story, this occasion also provided an opportunity to place many of Jesus' words and actions in the perspective of God's eternal purposes. For this reason they merit careful study as a means of interpreting not only what happened but also why it happened.

This important segment of John's Gospel reaches a climax in the eloquent prayer from which our lesson is taken. It has often been called Jesus' high-priestly prayer because He consecrated Himself as the sacrifice for the sins of the world and also consecrated His disciples to His service. This prayer is uniquely His.

What relevance does the prayer have for us today? Perhaps it can prompt us to think more seriously about some of the barriers we all raise to Christian unity—and move us to remedial action.

Light on the Text

Jesus Prays for Himself (17:1-5)

The prayer of John 17 follows the farewell discourses of Jesus in the Upper Room and reflects a similar frame of mind. We cannot be certain of the actual setting (depending on when 14:31c was carried out), but it was probably in the place where the Last Supper was eaten or somewhere along the way to the Kidron Valley and the olive grove beyond, where Jesus was betrayed and arrested.

Jesus was acutely aware of this moment, this "hour," that had come at last. Soon He would give of Himself sacrificially upon the cross. His choice had already been made. It was evident in the direction of His public ministry. He had alluded to the cross in His teachings and more recently He had "resolutely set out for Jerusalem" (Lk. 9:51) with full knowledge of what awaited Him. It was a critical moment for Him—and for all humanity—and so in these last hours of companionship with His friends, He dedicated Himself utterly to His Father, praying first for Himself, then for others.

One word appears several times in Jesus' prayer but in different forms. It is the noun "glory," or a form of the verb "glorify." Jesus was not talking about the glory we associate with celebrity. He was not seeking acclaim or demanding His rights. Jesus knew that glorifying God meant fulfilling God's work upon the cross. This had been His task on earth, a task He was about to complete (vs. 4). We must surely believe that He was also looking ahead to the glory of the Resurrection and beyond. The cross would seem to be utterly inglorious; Christ entreated the Father to reveal its ultimate glory. But the meaning is clear that we also glorify God when, like Jesus, we participate sacrificially in God's work in the world.

Our work, then, should be closely bound up with what Jesus was about throughout his ministry—giving life in its fullest, richest dimension to everyone who would listen and accept. We should remember that the key

63

desire of Christ was that we have eternal life—that we know God as the one, true God, and accept the revelation of God in Christ.

Jesus Prays for His Disciples (17:6-19)

Verse 6 is a brief summary statement at the beginning of Jesus' compassionate prayer for His disciples. Having prayed for Himself, our Lord next prayed for those close friends and companions who were present while He was speaking. Jesus had revealed "the only true God" to His disciples and they had freely accepted and obeyed God's word. They knew the Father because they had been with the Son. They also knew the Son because they believed He was sent by the Father. Therefore, Jesus was glorified through their obedient faith.

Verse 11 reveals the compassionate heart of Jesus: He was going home to His Father, and His followers would be left behind. This reminds us of the struggle that Paul had when he wrote, "I am torn between the two: I desire to depart and be with Christ, which is better by far; but it is more necessary for you that I remain in the body" (Phil. 1:23, 24). Jesus could not remain, so He prayed "Holy Father, protect them by the power of your name—the name you gave me." God's name refers to all His revealed character, and that same name is shared with the Son. The oneness shared by the Father and the Son is desired for the disciples as well. While Jesus was with them He could protect and unify them by the power of His presence. But since they received the truth of who God is in their lives, the whole world had turned against them and this hatred threatened their unity. Satan's flaming arrows were sent out to divide and conquer—to destroy their faith and solidarity towards God.

Jesus prays not only for their protection, but also for their purity. His disciples are no longer part of the world system, because they now are part of the Kingdom of Heaven. Since Jesus is not of the world His followers stand with Him against the world. Therefore, He prays that the Father would sanctify them—set them apart as sacred—by the truth, which is the Word of God. Likewise, "Christ loved the church and gave himself up for her to make her holy, cleansing her by the washing with water through the word" (Eph. 5:25, 26). Once they have been sanctified by the power of God's Word, then they are ready to go back into the world, undaunted by Satan's schemes, to "declare his glory among the nations" (Ps. 96:3).

Jesus Prays for All Believers (17:20-26)

When we think about Jesus on the cross, we see Him not just as a Savior for a particular group of followers at one moment in history, but as the world's Redeemer. We visualize His arms stretched out, even at the time of greatest pain and suffering, to encompass our entire globe.

His prayer has the same universal character. It transcends time and place to include present and future believers. There are several significant themes in this concluding segment of John 17.

1. Jesus' intercession for all who would later believe is so phrased that it continues to be relevant to every Christian—and each congregation of believers. There is neither a cutoff time nor any geographical limit. We are entitled, as current followers of Christ, to regard His prayer as intended for us. This assures us of His continuing concern for us. But it also requires that we take seriously what His prayer means for our life with fellow Christians.

2. The unity Jesus desired was not some kind of superficial togetherness. He prayed that we have the same intensity, the same continuity, the same intimacy, the same spiritual "oneness" He enjoyed in His communion with the Father. Believers are drawn to a unity that already exists in Christ, who provides a source, a base, a center for the Church's common life.

3. The unity Jesus prayed for has a larger purpose than stirring our hearts with a feeling of friendliness for each other. It ought to help the whole world know and accept the Gospel of Christ.

4. Several times in this chapter Jesus referred to His disciples and others who would heed His word as persons who were "given" Him by God. Those who are so given are the persons who hear the invitation that God issues in Christ and, having heard, respond to that

65

call. The "given" receive eternal life (vs. 2), are prayed for (vs. 9), have been guarded and kept by Jesus (vs. 12), and are promised a share of His glory (vs. 24).

For Discussion

1. As you meditate on the glory of the Father and the Son, consider how God's glory is made evident in your life. How has Jesus' completed work on the cross brought glory to the Father? To you?

2. Jesus had made the Father known to His disciples and they accepted the Father's words. They in turn declare God's Word down through the ages through the Bible, which is our basis for unity today. Why does Jesus pray for you to be one with other believers? How, in practical ways, is that unity actually carried out?

3. The world does not know the righteous Father, but the Lord Jesus promises to continue revealing the Father. Therefore, those who believe in Jesus will experience God's love and Christ's presence in their lives. How do you express the love of God in your worship of the Father? In your actions with other believers?

4. How can you cultivate an attitude of oneness with those of different Christian backgrounds? On what common grounds of faith and practice can Christians unite for worship and witness?

Window on the Word

The Love of Christ Binds Us

We had come together from many nations. The setting for our service was the small chapel of one of the evangelical academies in Germany, and most of the participants were German. But among the others were a Dutch Reformed seminarian, and some young Lutherans from Sweden. Joining in our discussions were a Greek Orthodox professor and a Russian Orthodox editor.

The speaker was Dr. F. M. Dobias, from Prague, Czechoslovakia, a professor and minister in the Church of the Bohemian Brethren. Because he would speak in German I expected to grasp only a few phrases of his message.

But almost from the moment he announced his text, the movement of his thought carried me along. A phrase from Paul's second letter to the Corinthians summarized it easily: "For Christ's love compels us," according to the New International Version, or "constraineth us" in the familiar King James translation. The speaker, however, was not satisfied to use the resources of only one language. In Greek and Latin, in German and French, in English and in the Slavic tongues, he approached the same idea, allowing each shading of language to throw a new light on the way the universal love of Christ takes hold of us, compelling, constraining, binding us together and to Him.

The love of Christ binds us. He is one Lord, and He carries no labels limiting Him to East or West, to one side rather than another, to one denomination over another, to one formula set against another. If the love of Christ constrains and controls us, and if we accept the mastery of that one Lord, we must be drawn together.

(Adapted from an editorial in *Messenger*, 1967.)

10

The Way of Holiness

Truth to Apply: Since I have died with Christ, the power of sin and death has been broken, and the Holy Spirit now empowers me to live a holy life.

Key Verse: Through Christ Jesus the law of the Spirit of life set me free from the law of sin and death (Rom. 8:2).

Simeon Stylites had gained a reputation for holiness by dressing in a hair shirt and living for years on top of a high pillar. Simeon would spend his time in prayer and meditation, like other religious ascetics of the early Middle Ages. These "pillar saints" wanted to purify their souls by doing penance for their sins on top of high columns.

Anatole of France was deeply impressed by this and desired to emulate St. Simeon. However, there were no pillars available, so he decided to use a chair on top of the kitchen table in his home. There he sat in the most uncomfortable clothes he could find, intending to spend the rest of his days in fasting and prayer.

The cook, as well as the rest of the family, could not understand the loftiness of his intentions. They did succeed, though, in making life miserable for him, so much so that he finally discontinued his project. In reflection, Anatole wrote these profound words: "Then I perceived that it is a very difficult thing to be a saint while living with your own family. I saw why Jerome went into the desert."

What is your own experience with attempts at personal holiness?

Background/Overview: *Romans 8:1-17*

The Epistle to the Romans has been called a Christian manifesto. According to the apostle Paul, each member of the human race is subject to sin's slavery. As we read this book, we may hear the clatter of emotional and spiritual chains everywhere we turn. But—and this is Paul's message—Jesus Christ came to set people free. Christ releases us from the bondage of guilt and self-centeredness, which keeps us from becoming fully human.

Romans 8, majestic in every way, pictures the Christian walking in the full freedom of Christ's salvation. From beginning to end, the chapter sounds the triumphant note of life lived on a level higher than world-minded people. What is the secret? Paul declares, "The law of the Spirit of life set me free from the law of sin and death" (Rom. 8:2).

British scholar W. H. Griffith Thomas calls Romans 8 "the chapter of chapters for the life of the believer" and quotes Spener as having said, "If Holy Scripture was a ring, and the Epistle to the Romans a precious stone, chapter 8 would be the sparkling point of the jewel."

In Romans 6—8 Paul sets forth the way of holiness, through the freeing power of Christ Jesus' death and resurrection. Chapter 6 emphasizes freedom from sin; chapter 7 stresses freedom from the law; and chapter 8 brings into focus freedom from death. The Holy Spirit does not figure prominently in Paul's exposition in 6 and 7, being mentioned only once (7:6). But in chapter 8, Paul refers to the Spirit 19 times. John Stott, in *Men Made New,* has summarized the activity of the Holy Spirit in four areas: "He subdues our flesh (vss. 5-13); He witnesses to our sonship (vss. 14-17); He guarantees our inheritance (vss. 18-25); and He helps our weakness in prayer (vss. 26, 27)." Paul recognized the power of sin; but he also recognized the greater power of the Spirit, whom God has given His children. It is the Holy Spirit who gives life to our spirits, and who will finally give life to our resurrected bodies. Approach the study of this passage, then, as an exercise in learning just how powerful your resources for holy living really are!

Light on the Text

Holiness Made Possible (8:1-4)

Those who are outside of Christ are "condemned already because (they have) not believed in the name of God's one and only Son" (Jn. 3:18). But for those who are in Christ there is now no declaration of guilt. Why? Because of two reasons: (1) Christ's death on the cross paid for our crimes against God, so our guilt has been removed; and (2) we have died with Christ, hence we have died to sin, so we are no longer bound by the law of sin and death. For example, when someone passes away, that person is no longer affected by the laws of the earthbound universe—his or her spirit is free. Likewise, when someone dies with Christ, that person is no longer affected by the law of sin and death—the spirit is set free by a new law, the law of the Spirit. Therefore, we are able to live a holy life, because the power of sin and guilt has been rendered powerless.

Verse 3 states that the Mosaic Law was powerless to overcome the law of sin and death. In fact it was weakened by our sinful nature. How? Paul explains that "when the commandment came, sin sprang to life and I died. I found that the very commandment that was intended to bring life actually brought death" (7:9, 10). This is the paradox that Paul is alluding to here in verse 3 of chapter 8: the Mosaic Law was given so someone could know how to live a holy life, but as Paul says, "sin, seizing the opportunity afforded by the commandment, deceived me, and through the commandment put me to death" (7:11). In reality the sinful nature makes the Mosaic Law impossible to fulfill, because the Law only arouses sinful passions to the extent of doing evil even when the desire is to do good (cf. 7:5, 15-20). What a dilemma!

But "Thanks be to God—through Jesus Christ our Lord!" God overcame the Law of sin and death "by sending his own Son in the likeness of sinful man to be a sin offering." Jesus' death and resurrection broke the power of sin and death. Now the sinner in Christ is no longer condemned. Therefore, it is now possible to live a

71

holy life to meet "the righteous requirements of the law" (vs. 4). The sinner in Christ has been set free by "the law of the Spirit of life" to live a life of obedience which leads to holiness.

Holiness Made Practical (8:5-11)

Knowing that Christ Jesus has rendered sin powerless in my life is a marvelous truth, but what are some practical steps I can follow that lead to holiness? God has freed me from the power of sin, but what must I do to experience this freedom? Paul gives us two steps: one involves the mind, and the other, the will.

In verses 5 to 7, the word "mind[s]" is used five times, which emphasizes the great importance of the way one thinks with respect to holiness. Paul simply compares the spiritual mind with the sinful mind. Those who live according to their sinful passions set their minds on what feels good. Personal pleasure is all they can think about, to the point of no return. James clearly explains, "each one is tempted when, by his own evil desire, he is dragged away and enticed. Then, after desire has conceived, it gives birth to sin; and sin, when it is full-grown, gives birth to death" (Jas. 1:14, 15). Temptation begins with the mind, then it plays on one's affections, until the conscience of the person becomes useless.

Those who live according to the Spirit, however, set their minds on what the Spirit desires. Their thoughts are not controlled by their feelings, but "by the Spirit [of] life and peace." The sinful mind is hostile toward God and leads to death. The spiritual is at peace with God (cf. 5:1), which leads to eternal life. Paul later commands "Do not conform any longer to the pattern of this world, but be transformed by the renewing of your mind" (12:2). The pattern of this world has already been set in our minds by our sinful nature; now we must repattern our thinking according to the Word of God. Step number one is to take our minds off of our feelings, and start pondering what pleases the Spirit.

Step number two has to do with our will. Verses 8 and 9 speak about who is in control. If we allow our sinful passions to rule our lives, we can in no way please God. But, if we allow the Holy Spirit to control us, we can discern what God's will is. This is a matter of choice. Who is going to be the boss in your life? Your feelings? Or the Spirit of God? Who do you belong to anyway? "You are not your own; you were bought at a price" (I Cor. 6:19, 20). You belong to Christ, and your body is the temple of the Holy Spirit. Therefore, decide right now to let Christ be Lord in your life, not just a guest who is forgotten or shunned.

Holiness Made Personal (8:12-17)

Paul begins this section by addressing his brothers and sisters in Christ. He calls on their sense of duty to no longer live according to the sinful nature, but urges them to live according to the Spirit. They are obligated to do so because of all Christ has done in giving them spiritual life now (vs. 10), and promising eternal life in the future (vs. 11). What does their obligation involve? Verse 13 says to "put to death the misdeeds of the body." This means to simply stop giving into one's sinful desires. This is every believer's duty; we are no longer slaves to sin but slaves "to obedience, which leads to righteousness" (6:16). We have an obligation to obey God.

Paul appeals to our sense of duty, not only as slaves of God, but as sons of God. Usually the concept of slavery induces the aura of fear and cruelty. So, Paul portrays a more intimate relationship of father and son, rather than master and slave. If we are led by the Spirit of God, then we have "received the Spirit of sonship" or adoption. As John states, "Yet to all who received him, [Christ], to those who believed in his name, he gave the right to become children of God . . . born of God" (Jn. 1:12, 13). The Holy Spirit also gives witness to us that we are God's children and heirs. Therefore, we are truly obligated to live according to the Spirit of God, because we are now His obedient children.

For Discussion

1. Many times we are tempted and fall into sin. It becomes discouraging when we feel trapped in the same

pattern of our error time after time. How does the fact that Christ's death rendered sin powerless encourage you when tempted?

2. What we fill our minds with is vital in our pursuit of holiness. In what way have your feelings and natural desires been controlling your thinking? What steps could you take to renew your thinking patterns to be more conformed to God's Word?

3. Submission to anybody's authority except to our own is not very popular today. In fact, submitting to God is the last thing most of us care to think about. Is the Spirit in control of your attitudes and actions? In what ways has God's Spirit been exercising control over your life recently?

4. How is a slave obligated to obey his master? A son to obey his father? Do you have this same sense of duty when it comes to living in accordance with the Spirit? How is holiness going to be a priority in your life from now on? (See I Pet. 1:14, 15.)

Window on the Word

I Will Not Abandon You

In the days of the three-masted schooners, the signal flags "B.N.G." meant "I will not abandon you." This was one of the most important messages a ship could send as it drew alongside a distressed vessel. Here was a promise of help and encouragement—word that a friend was near.

In much the same way, the Holy Spirit comes alongside us in our moments of weakness and despair, and signals hope to distressed believers everywhere. Though we may be "sinking deep in sin far from the peaceful shore," the Spirit of God leads us in the way of holiness back to the loving care of the Father.

(Adapted from a story in *The Miracle of the Cross*, by Robert R. Brown)

11

The Most Excellent Way

Truth to Apply: When I exercise my God-given gift in the Body of Christ, I am called to serve out of a deep love for others.

Key Verse: Eagerly desire the greater gifts. And now I will show you the most excellent way (I Cor. 12:31).

When Wycliffe translator Doug Meland and his wife moved into a village of Brazil's Fulnio Indians, he was referred to simply as "the white man." The term was by no means complimentary, since other white men had exploited them, burned their homes, and robbed them of their lands.

But after the Melands learned the Fulnio language and began to help the people with medicine and in other ways, they began calling Doug "the respectable white man."

When the Melands began adapting the customs of the people, the Fulnio gave them greater acceptance and spoke of Doug as "the white Indian."

Then one day, as Doug was washing the dirty, blood-caked foot of an injured Fulnio boy, he overheard a bystander say to another: "Whoever heard of a white man washing an Indian's foot before? Certainly this man is from God!" From that day on whenever Doug would go into an Indian home, it would be announced: "Here comes the man God sent us."

Have you ever had your feet washed—either literally, or symbolically? How did you feel?

First-century Corinth was a brawling waterway city of what we call Greece. This bustling, cosmopolitan center overflowed with religions, some so depraved that the Roman government refused to license them.

Corinthian morals were so low that if you mentioned the city's name, someone might respond with a knowing snicker. The inhabitants were materialistic pleasure-seekers—a hard lot to evangelize.

Yet, in spite of its bad reputation, Corinth was in some ways actually an ideal city to evangelize. Ships from all over the known world passed through the nearby Isthmus of Corinth, and the Isthmian Games drew throngs of Romans. Paul probably realized that if he could start a church in Corinth, Christianity would soon spread to other parts of the Roman Empire as well.

For 18 months, Paul evangelized the city and formed his converts into a small church. After he left, Apollos, an eloquent preacher from Alexandria, Egypt, continued his work. Some time later, Paul heard disturbing reports about problems in the church—factions, immorality, and legal battles. Several Corinthians wrote to him, seeking advice about marriage, celibacy, and other matters.

Paul's answer has come down to us as I Corinthians, a long disciplinary letter pointing out the church's flaws and directing them toward Christian maturity.

In Chapters 12, 13, and 14, Paul discusses the proper use of spiritual gifts within the context of public worship (chaps. 11—14).

Light on the Text

The Context of Love (12:27-31)

God gave the Church gifts, but He didn't intend for them to become trophies. This is precisely what happened in the Corinthian fellowship. Some members with spiritual insight felt superior about what they knew. Others felt the ability to speak in tongues or perform miraculous healings were the greatest gifts. These Christians were spotlight stealers. Instead of realizing they were part of a big cast, they tried to steal the whole show.

Paul argued for a larger vision. "Think big!" he said. "The Church is more than one gift or even several. It is the total group, all working together for the common good."

Paul then cataloged the spiritual gifts God had granted the Church. He gave some the ability to communicate the faith: apostles, prophets, and teachers. He granted other people gifts of supernatural power: workers of miracles, healers, tongues, and interpreters. He gave still other gifts that contributed toward an efficient-running organization: helpers and administrators. No one possessed all these gifts, and no gift was shared by everyone.

Paul's emphasis throughout was unity. Just as all the organs in the human body must work together, he reasoned, so the Church must function as a single, living unit. How could this take place? Chapter 12 ends almost in a whisper, as if Paul were beckoning his listeners to bend an ear and listen to a godly secret. He would tell the Church in chapter 13 of an even higher goal—"the most excellent way."

The Constraint of Love (13:1-3)

We often think of love as the oil in the machinery of the Church, without which members rub against each other, sparking discord and thus hindering the Lord's work. This notion, while interesting, actually places love in a secondary rather than a primary role. Love is not merely the lubricant of the Church machine; *love is the work of the Church,* the primary ingredient.

To emphasize love's centrality in the Church, Paul told his readers that love is indispensable. Everything that springs from the heart of a child of God ought to be characterized by love. Without it, Paul said, the most eloquent speaking is just so much noise. In Paul's day cymbals were used in the worship of Dionysus and other gods. The Corinthian Christians would have understood this as a jarring comparison with local pagan worship.

Paul was without doubt one of the keenest Christian teachers of the day. Yet he realized that even if he knew the deepest mysteries of God's plans and purposes and could astound the world with his faith, he would still amount to nothing if he acted without love.

A person might give away all his possessions to feed the poor and even forfeit his life for the faith; yet without love, giving away everything in one grand gesture means nothing. True love does not need a supreme crisis in order to function. True love manifests itself every day in ordinary circumstances.

The Content of Love (13:4-7)

Most people carry an identification card of some sort, whether it's a driver's license, a student card, or employee badge. These handy devices condense a lot of vital information into a small space.

Paul's description of Christian love is as efficient as an I.D. card. His 14 concise statements quickly set apart godly love from its imitators.

Several of the qualities here have to do with greatness. People who love as God loves have greatness of heart, sometimes called a magnanimous spirit. If someone tells you John Doe is a great man, the comment may have nothing to do with height or weight, but refers to excellence of character.

The Corinthian church needed mature Christians. When Paul wrote "love is patient, love is kind," he was appealing for restraint and gentle action. Mature people don't explode at the rudeness of other persons; they keep on being gentle, keep on being kind.

In verse 5, Paul expressed the same idea in negative terms: love "is not easily angered, it keeps no record of wrongs." Loving people don't fly off the handle quickly when someone steps on their egos. They endure minor irritations without flaring. It takes a big person to forgive consistently and not tabulate the offenses of others. But this is the way God's love is. Love doesn't keep a ledger of wrongs received, crossing them off only when necessary. Love forgives.

The mature person "does not delight in evil but rejoices with the truth" (vs. 6). Just as love refuses to store up injuries, so it also refuses to relish the downfall of others. A big person doesn't delight in listening to scandal or spreading gossip; rather, he or she is always eager to bring out the best in people. Paul used the word truth in its broadest sense: good as opposed to unrighteousness. A loving person is on God's side and is always encouraging righteousness in others.

If love means greatness, it can also mean humility. Contradictory? No, for Paul made it clear that love is often found in the lowly, humble ways of life.

For example, love "does not envy" (vs. 4). Few of Paul's converts were wealthy or wise; most belonged to the lower and uneducated class of artisans and shopkeepers. There may have been slaves in the church who envied those who were free. Paul pointed out that those who love are content with what they have. They are not jealous of those who have more.

As for those who brag or expect preferential treatment, Paul said, love "does not boast, it is not proud" (vs. 4). We might say, "Love keeps us from getting bigheaded; love recognizes our limitations and our need for others."

Paul also admonished those whose rudeness ruined church gatherings. Humble people are sensitive to other people's feelings. Instead of thinking only of themselves, they try not to offend.

Paul also said that love "is not self-seeking" (vs. 5). Arrogant people insist upon having their way. Their self-importance prevents them from considering other people's needs. Love humbles them so that they think of everyone's good, not just their own.

Paul summarized love's essence in verse 7: love protects, trusts, hopes, and perseveres in all things. Those who love persist in believing that God will prevail. In spite of persecution and disappointment, love keeps on hoping, keeps on doing good.

The Continuity of Love (13:8-13)

One of the most distressing things about life is its transience. Homes need continual repair, newly purchased lawn mowers break down, and clothes quickly go out of style. It's discouraging to plunk down several thousand dollars for a car with a two-year warranty.

We all want to latch onto things that last, but how? Paul directed his people to the enduring qualities of love, saying, "Love never fails."

The Greek word for "fail" appears in other ancient writings to describe the fading of flowers. Paul meant that love never fades—it is indestructible.

Paul valued prophecy. He also valued knowledge and the gift of tongues. But none of these gifts are eternal, he said. Each will one day give way to the surpassing excellence of love.

Next, Paul used the analogy of growing up to explain the transience of spiritual gifts. He said that when he was a child, he spoke, thought, and understood "like a child." These three verbs parallel tongues, prophecy, and knowledge. What he meant was that these gifts would eventually outgrow their usefulness just as childlike traits ultimately give way to maturity. They are transient, while love is permanent.

Third, Paul compared love's excellence to seeing "face to face," as opposed to looking "in a mirror," which gives a "poor reflection." We will one day have immediate contact with God, surpassing even what Moses enjoyed (Num. 12:8). Then we will know, or have understanding, just as fully as we are known by Him. We do not have this kind of perception now, even with the help of our spiritual gifts.

Paul concluded his prose poem on love by pointing out three of the top virtues in the Christian life—faith, hope, and love. His phrase "and now these three remain" may possibly refer to the present age or to eternity. Whether all three virtues have an eternal life span or not, love is the greatest. Love is equally at home in this age and the next. Love is never outgrown. Love has an eternal pledge.

For Discussion

1. The Body of Christ has many parts, yet it should work as a whole. In what ways might you foster an attitude of interdependence in your own local church?

2. Paul reveals that the most excellent way to serve others in the Body is with a genuine attitude of love. How would you evaluate your own performance in this regard? What needs to be changed?

3. Love is active. Verse 7 lists four verbs that describe love as being responsible. How can you demonstrate your love toward other believers in the Body of Christ in these four ways?

Window on the Word

Love is not blind—it sees more, not less. But because it sees more, it is willing to see less.
  (Rabbi Julius Gordon)

12
Spiritual Fitness

Truth to Apply: For spiritual fitness, I must learn to exercise the unity of the Spirit.

Key Verse: From him the whole body, joined and held together by every supporting ligament, grows and builds itself up in love, as each part does its work (Eph. 4:16).

Zuver's Gym and Muscle Hall of Fame in Costa Mesa, California, has to be one of a kind. And the same goes for its owner, Bob Zuver, an ordained minister and former weight lifter, who originated and built the gym and its equipment. He says that it's a "fun place to work out."

Inside the heavy iron gate stands a fearsome-looking fiberglass gorilla. Not far away are a ten-foot superman and a fiberglass elephant lifting a barbell with its trunk. The door leading into the main gym weighs two tons!

Everything inside is big. There are a one thousand-pound "blob," and several unique racks. Bells ring and lights flash when they are lifted. There is also the world's biggest drinking fountain—a fire hydrant!

The main purpose of the gym is to build fitness and strength, not only physically but spiritually, too. The Church is also like a gym—a spiritual gym. According to the apostle Paul, we all are commanded: "train yourself to be godly. For physical training is of some value, but godliness has value for all things, holding promise for both the present life and the life to come" (I Tim. 4:7, 8).

In what ways have you found discipline to be an important factor in your spiritual growth?

Ephesians is one of Paul's prison epistles (i.e., he was in prison when he wrote them). It, along with several other letters, was sent to Christians at Ephesus and at other cities in Asia Minor to defend the integrity of Christian living amid the gross idolatry of pagan culture. Today's passage is a high point.

The city of Ephesus was among the most important religious centers in all Asia Minor. It was a crossroads of communication, commerce, and craftsmanship—especially the trade of silversmithing and idol making (Acts 19:23-28).

The cosmopolitan mood of Ephesus welcomed various philosophies and religions, most notably the cult of Diana, the Roman fertility goddess associated with the moon and hunting. Worshipers of Diana believed that she, along with other gods, exerted influence over mankind and that life could be more pleasant and profitable if they pleased her. Sacrifices were made to her for that reason.

Paul confronted this cult and opposed it vigorously on his third missionary journey. His defense—partly preserved in Ephesians—was a key reason for the spread of Christianity.

In Ephesians 1—3, Paul stressed the believer's rich spiritual standing in Jesus Christ. Beginning with chapter 4, the apostle exhorted his readers to translate that spiritual wealth into daily living, drawing upon the strength of the empowered Body of Christ.

Paul's words were a source of much strength and encouragement. In our day—with such anxious searching for true faith—the truth of Ephesians still stands. Jesus Christ is Lord of all. He alone deserves our worship, love, and daily devotion.

Light on the Text

Exercising Unity (4:1-6)

Paul, writing from prison, urged those not in physical

chains to be unified—united as tightly as possible according to the working of the Holy Spirit.

The first part of this Scripture passage teaches the organic identity of the Christian body. A physical body is harmoniously constructed and unified; all parts operate smoothly for the welfare of the whole. Christian unity is strengthened as we realize who we are in Christ and what is expected of us.

Paul implored the Ephesians to walk worthy of their calling as Christians, and to stay united in belief and action. He pleaded strongly with them because unity was so vital to the growth of the Church.

Christians sometimes overlook the importance of the New Testament's teaching concerning the Church as the Body of Christ. It's easy to think of the Church only as some voluntary association like a lodge, club, or social agency. But that is not essentially what the Church is. It is a living, functioning body animated (made alive) by one Spirit. The Church has a singular calling and a shared hope. Its members are to represent—and present—Christ to the world. That is their chief mission.

There is no time for sloth and no room for divisiveness, Paul urged. A joint mission challenges all Christians to do what they can to spread the love of Christ. Everyone who has committed his life to Christ can make an effective contribution toward this end. Appreciating one another's gifts is a necessary beginning.

Exercising Grace (4:7-13)

The second part of the text explains the organic functioning of the Church. Everyone has a part to play, and each person's gifts are to be used in harmony to help the total body to mature in Christlikeness.

Other New Testament passages speak of the body of Christians in terms of the unity they should show. John 17 (see chap. 9) presents a message of Christian unity in terms of the singleness of purpose Christians should display in accomplishing the will of God. Jesus prayed, concerning all believers in every age, "that all of them may be one" (17:21). Nothing should obscure that fact in the minds and lives of all Christians.

In I Corinthians 12 the emphasis differs slightly. Unity

is illustrated in terms of the absolute interdependence of the many parts of a single body. Every part needs every other part in order to form a healthy body.

Ephesians 4 gives a third meaning to Christian unity. It is expressed in terms of shared goals that, when accomplished, contribute to the growth of the body.

One goal is to achieve "unity in the faith" (vs. 13). This means coming to a point where Christ is central in all our living and teaching. Another goal is unity "in the knowledge of the Son of God." When this goal is achieved, believers are more closely identifiable with Christ. They are more mature in their outlook and behavior. They know what Christ expects and they live up to His expectations.

Different gifts and leadership roles have been assigned by the Lord to enhance unity and maturity among Christ's body.

This is important. Too often the administration of gifts and leadership abilities directs attention to the ones exercising the gifts and acting in leadership roles. More true to New Testament teaching is the concern to edify and perfect the body of believers, and to promote the work of the ministry. Simply stated, the Lord has placed certain people in certain positions because that is where they can best be used by Him to build up His Body.

Exercising Truth (4:14-16)

The third part of this passage deals with the Body of Christ maturing by "speaking the truth in love." Paul initially describes the spiritual "infant" that is "tossed back and forth" and "blown here and there," like a ship on the high seas. This person is easily influenced by all kinds of teaching, inside and outside the church, which is not based on the truth—namely Christ and His words. As Homer A. Kent, Jr. observes: "The great danger to immature faith is false doctrine; it is here compared to strong winds which toss about an unguided boat. Such false doctrine is always being promoted by crafty men who by trickery and scheming lead their victims into spiritual disaster" (*Ephesians: The Glory of the Church*, Moody Press, Chicago, 1971).

Full maturity in Christ must therefore be attained by

speaking and acting in absolute truthfulness. The great problem, though, is that the spiritually immature are quickly enticed by heretical doctrine and unworthy conduct. Therefore, we must speak the truth in love "so that they may have the full riches of complete understanding, in order that they may know the mystery of God, namely, Christ, in whom are hidden all the treasures of wisdom and knowledge" (Col. 2:2, 3). Furthermore, Paul emphasizes that all truth should be expressed "in love." Christ as the Head guides the whole body to grow and build itself up "in love." Truth must never be sacrificed in the interests of love, but it must always be maintained in a spirit of love.

Obviously we cannot grow by taking it easy, especially if we accept Paul's teaching on the properly working church. Maturity involves hard work—the spiritual exercise of serving others and receiving the service of others as we worship our Lord.

For Discussion

1. Paul exhorts us to exercise the unity of the Spirit by humility, gentleness, and patience. Have you ever been harsh or impatient with one who is weak in the faith? How can you "make every effort" to restore and keep the unity of the Spirit in these relationships?

2. Christ has given us gifts to build solidarity in the church. What do you sense is your gift, and how do you specifically use it to prepare others for service or to meet others' needs? Describe how exercising your gift builds the body up towards unity and maturity in Christ.

3. Do you know of someone who needs your loving concern for what that person believes or does? Ask God to give you the words and the opportunity to confront this one in love.

4. In Ephesians 6:11 we are exhorted to "put on the full armor of God" in order to stand against temptation. What does this mean for you in your daily living? Do you have any advice for others from your own experience with overcoming such temptation?

Window on the Word

Fit and Alive at 85

On his 85th birthday, John Wesley wrote in his diary these rephrased lines:

"I find some decay in my memory with regard to names and things lately past, but not at all with what I had read 20, 40, or 60 years ago. Nor do I feel any weariness, either in traveling or preaching. To what cause can I impute this? First, to the power of God, fitting me to the work to which I am called; and next to the prayers of His children. Then, may not I also impute it to these inferior means:

1. My constant exercise and change of air;
2. My never having lost a night's sleep, sick or well, on land or at sea;
3. My having slept at command, whether day or night;
4. My having risen constantly at 4:00 AM for about 60 years;
5. My constant preaching at 5:00 AM for above 50 years; and
6. My having so little pain, sorrow, or anxious care in life."

(Journal of John Wesley)

Leader Helps and Lesson Plan

General Guidelines for Group Study

*Open and close each session with prayer.

*Since the lesson texts are not printed in the book, group members should have their Bibles with them for each study session.

*As the leader, prepare yourself for each session through personal study (during the week) of the Bible text and lesson. On notepaper, jot down any points of interest or concern as you study. Jot down your thoughts about how God is speaking to you through the text, and how He might want to speak to the entire group. Look up cross-reference passages (as they are referred to in the lessons), and try to find answers to questions that come to your mind. Also, recall stories from your own life experience that could be shared with the group to illustrate points in the lesson.

*Try to get participation from everyone. Get to know the more quiet members through informal conversation before and after the sessions. Then, during the study, watch for nonverbal signs (a change in expression or posture) that they would like to respond. Call on them. Say: "What are your thoughts on this, Sue?"

*Don't be afraid of silence. Adults need their own space. Often a long period of silence after a question means the group has been challenged to do some real thinking—hard work that can't be rushed!

*Acknowledge each contribution. No question is a dumb question. Every comment, no matter how "wrong," comes from a worthy person, who needs to be affirmed as valuable to the group. Find ways of tactfully accepting the speaker while guiding the discussion back on track: "Thank you for that comment, John; now what do some of the others think?" or, "I see your point, but are you aware of . . . ?"

When redirecting the discussion, however, be sensitive to the fact that sometimes the topic of the moment *should be* the "sidetrack" because it hits a felt need of the participants.

*Encourage *well-rounded* Christian growth. Christians are called to grow in knowledge of the Word, but they are also challenged to grow in love and wisdom. This means that they must constantly develop in their ability to wisely apply the Bible knowledge to their experience.

Lesson Plan

The following four-step lesson plan can be used effectively for each chapter, varying the different suggested approaches from lesson to lesson.

STEP 1: *Focus on Life Need*

The opening section of each lesson is an anecdote, quote, or other device designed to stimulate sharing on how the topic relates to practical daily living. There are many ways to do this. For example, you might list on the chalkboard the group's answers to: "How have you found this theme relevant to your daily life?" "What are your past successes, or failures, in this area?" "What is your present level of struggle or victory with this?" "Share a story from your own experience relating to this topic."

Sharing questions are designed to be open-ended and allow people to talk about themselves. The questions allow for sharing about past experiences, feelings, hopes and dreams, fears and anxieties, faith, daily life, likes and dislikes, sorrows and joys. Self-disclosure results in group members' coming to know each other at a more intimate level. This kind of personal sharing is necessary to experience deep affirmation and love.

However you do it, the point is to get group members to share *where they are now* in relation to the Biblical topic. As you seek to get the group involved, remember the following characteristics of good sharing questions:[1]

1. Good sharing questions encourage risk without forcing participants to go beyond their willingness to respond.

2. Good sharing questions begin with low risk and build toward higher risk. (It is often good, for instance, to ask a history question to start, then build to present situations in people's lives.)

3. Sharing questions should not require people to confess their sins or to share only negative things about themselves.

4. Questions should be able to be answered by every member of the group.

5. The questions should help the group members to know one another better and learn to love and understand each other more.

6. The questions should allow for enough diversity in response so each member does not wind up saying the same thing.

7. They should ask for sharing of self, not for sharing of opinions.

STEP 2: *Focus on Bible Learning*

Use the "Light on the Text" section for this part of the lesson plan. Again, there are a number of ways to get group members involved, but the emphasis here is more on learning Bible content than on applying it. Below are some suggestions on how to proceed. The methods could be varied from week to week.

*Lecture on important points in the Bible passage (from your personal study notes).

*Assign specific verses in the Bible passage to individuals. Allow five or ten minutes for them to jot down 1) questions, 2) comments, 3) points of concern raised by the text. Then have them share in turn what they have written down.

*Pick important or controversial verses from the passage. In advance, do a personal study to find differences of interpretation among commentators. List and explain these "options" on a blackboard and invite comments concerning the relative merits of each view. Summarize and explain your own view, and challenge other group members to further study.

*Have class members do their own outline of the Bible passage. This is done by giving an original title to each section, chapter, and paragraph, placing each under its appropriate heading according to subject matter. Share the outlines and discuss.

*Make up your own sermons from the Bible passage. Each sermon could include: Title, Theme Sentence, Outline, Illustration, Application, Benediction. Share and discuss.

*View works of art based on the text. Discuss.

*Individually, or as a group, paraphrase the Bible passage in your own words. Share and discuss.

*Have a period of silent meditation upon the Bible passage. Later, share insights.

STEP 3: *Focus on Bible Application*

Most adults prefer group discussion above any other learning method. Use the "For Discussion" section for each lesson to guide a good discussion on the lesson topic and how it relates to felt needs.

Students can benefit from discussion in a number of important ways:[2]

1. Discussion stimulates interest and thinking, and helps students develop the skills of observation, analysis, and hope.

2. Discussion helps students clarify and review what they have learned.

3. Discussion allows students to hear opinions that are more mature and perhaps more Christlike than their own.

4. Discussion stimulates creativity and aids students in applying what they have learned.

5. When students verbalize what they believe and are forced to explain or defend what they say, their convictions are strengthened and their ability to share what they believe with others is increased.

There are many different ways to structure a discussion. All have group interaction as their goal. All provide an opportunity to share in the learning process.

But using different structures can add surprise to a discussion. It can mix people in unique ways. It can allow new people to talk.

Total Class Discussion

In some small classes, all students are able to participate in one effective discussion. This can build a sense of class unity, and it allows everyone to hear the wisdom of peers. But in most groups, total class discussion by itself is unsatisfactory because there is usually time for only a few to contribute.

Buzz Groups

Small groups of three to ten people are assigned any topic for discussion. They quickly select a chairperson and a secretary. The chairperson is responsible for keeping the discussion on track, and the secretary records the group's ideas, reporting the relevant ones to the total class.

Brainstorming

Students, usually in small groups, are presented with a problem and asked to come up with as many different solutions as possible. Participants should withhold judgment until all suggestions (no matter how creative!) have been offered. After a short break, the group should pick the best contribution from those suggested and refine it. Each brainstorming group will present its solution in a total class discussion.

Forum Discussion

Forum discussion is especially valuable when the subject is difficult and the students would not be able to participate in a meaningful discussion without quite a bit of background. People with special training or experience have insights which would not ordinarily be available to the students. Each forum member should prepare a three- to five-minute speech and be given uninterrupted time in which to present it. Then students should be encouraged to interact with the speakers, either directly or through a forum moderator.

Debate

As students prepare before class for their parts in a debate, they should remember that it is the affirmative side's responsibility to prove that the resolve is correct. The negative has to prove that it isn't. Of course, the negative may also want to present an alternative proposal.

There are many ways to structure a debate, but the following pattern is quite effective.
1. First affirmative speech
2. First negative speech
3. Second affirmative speech
4. Second negative speech
   (brief break while each side plans its rebuttal)
5. First negative rebuttal
6. First affirmative rebuttal
7. Second negative rebuttal
8. Second affirmative rebuttal.

Floating Panel

Sometimes you have a topic to which almost everyone in the room would have something to contribute, for example: marriage, love, work, getting along with people. For a change of pace, have a floating panel: four or five people, whose names are chosen at random, will become "experts" for several minutes. These people sit in chairs in the front of the room while you and other class members ask them questions. The questions should be experience related. When the panel has been in front for several minutes, enough time for each person to make several comments, draw other names and replace the original members.

Interview As Homework

Ask students to interview someone during the week and present what they learned in the form of short reports the following Sunday.

Interview in Class

Occasionally it is profitable to schedule an in-class interview, perhaps with a visiting missionary or with someone who has unique insights to share with the group. One person can take charge of the entire interview, structuring and asking questions. But whenever possible the entire class should take part. Each student should write a question to ask the guest.

In-Group Interview

Divide the class into groups of three, called triads. Supply all groups with the same question or discussion topic. A in the group interviews B while C listens. Then B interviews C while A listens. Finally C interviews A while B listens. Each interview should take from one to three minutes. When the triads return to the class, each person reports on what was heard rather than said.

Following every class period in which you use discussion, ask yourself these questions to help determine the success of your discussion time:

1. In what ways did this discussion contribute to the group's understanding of today's lesson?

2. If each person was not involved, what can I do next week to correct the situation?

3. In what ways did content play a role in the discussion? (I.e., people were not simply sharing off-the-top-of-their-head opinions.)

4. What follow-up, if any, should be made on the discussion? (For example, if participants showed a lack of knowledge, or misunderstanding in some area of Scripture, you may want to cover this subject soon during the class hour. Or, if they discussed decisions they were making or projects they felt the class should be involved in, follow-up outside the class hour may be necessary.)

STEP 4: *Focus on Life Response*

This step tries to incorporate a bridge from the Bible lesson to actual daily living. It should be a *specific* suggestion as to "how we are going to *do* something about this," either individually, or as a group. Though this is a goal to aim for, it is unlikely that everyone will respond to every lesson. But it is good to have a suggested life response ready for that one or two in the group who may have been moved by *this* lesson to respond *this week* in a tangible way.

Sometimes a whole group will be moved by one particular lesson to do a major project in light of their deepened understanding of, and commitment to, God's will. Such a response would be well worth the weeks of study that may have preceded it.

Examples of life response activities:

1. A whole class, after studying Scriptural principles of evangelism, decides to host an outreach Bible study in a new neighborhood.

2. As a result of studying one of Paul's prayers for the Ephesians, a group member volunteers to start and oversee a church prayer chain for responding to those in need.

3. A group member invites others to join her in memorizing the key verse for the week.

4. Two group members, after studying portions of the Sermon on the Mount, write and perform a song about peacemaking.

Obviously, only you and your group can decide how to respond appropriately to the challenge of living for Christ daily. But the possibilities are endless.

---

[1]From *Using the Bible in Groups,* by Roberta Hestenes.
© Roberta Hestenes 1983. Adapted and used by permission of Westminster Press, Philadelphia, PA.
[2]The material on discussion methods is adapted from *Creative Teaching Methods,* by Marlene D. LeFever, available from your local Christian bookstore or from David C. Cook Publishing Co., 850 N. Grove Ave., Elgin, IL 60120. Order number: 25254. $14.95. This book contains step-by-step directions for dozens of methods appropriate for use in adult classes.